LOGIRIDDLES

Logical Puzzles to Challenge Your Brain & Improve Your Aptitude

Group Captain D. P. Apte (Retd.)

VISHWAKARMA PUBLICATIONS
VP

Logiriddles

Logical Puzzles to Challenge Your Brain & Improve Your Aptitude

Second Edition - June 2015
© Group Captain D. P. Apte (Retd.)
dpapte54@gmail.com

ISBN 978-93-83572-73-1

All rights reserved. No part of this book will be reproduced, used or stored in any form without the prior permission of the Publisher.

Published by:
Vishwakarma Publications
283, Budhawar Peth, Near City Post,
Pune- 411 002.
Phone No: (020) 20261157
Email: info@vpindia.co.in
Website: www.vpindia.co.in

Cover Design
Meghnad Deodhar

Typeset and Layout
Gold Fish Graphics, Pune.

Printed at
**Repro Knowledgecast Limited
Thane**

LOGIRIDDLES

Logical Puzzles to Challenge Your Brain & Improve Your Aptitude

Group Captain D.P. Apte is Professor and Director of MIT School of Business, Pune, India, and mentor at MIT School of Government. He has more than 35 years of experience as an engineer, manager and teacher. He retired from the Indian Air Force in 2002, after 25 years of distinguished service as an engineer-manager. During this period he taught aerodynamics and propulsion engineeringat Air Force Technical College and other training institutes of IAF.

Since 2002 he has taught thousands of MCA and MBA students at various institutes in Pune. He teaches Quantitative Techniques, Operations Research, Statistical Methods, Research Methodology, Probability and Combinatorics subjects at post graduate level. He has successfully conducted a number of programs to generate interest in mathematics among students who do not like (rather hate) mathematics. As a corporate trainer he has conducted number of workshops and seminars for industry on various subjects.

He headed MIT School of Management, Pune from 2003 to 2009, and has been Director and Professor at MIT School of Business, Pune since 2009. He conducts motivational programs for students using Neuro Linguistic Programming (NLP) and also provides personal counseling for motivating people.

He is the author of ten books so far in the area of probability, combinatorics, statistics, operational research, quantitative techniques and Neuro Linguistic Programming (NLP). Among the awards he has received are a Gold medal at Crainfield University, 'Best Teacher Award' in 2009, Best Director Award in 2013, Distinguished Educator Award in 2014, and Shikshak Gaurav Puraskar 2014.

ACKNOWLEDGEMENT

I would like to express my sincere thanks to all those who directly or indirectly contributed to this book. Firstly, I would like to thank my student Trushal Rana who actually ignited me to write this book by asking my help to solve few challenging puzzles while he was preparing for placement interviews. I also wish to thank my daughter Mrs. Poorwa Joshi who cross-checked my answers and gave me valuable suggestions. I would like to express my sincere gratitude to my mother late Mrs. Usha Apte who is my inspiration.

I would also like to express my immense gratitude to Mr. Lakshman Iyer and staff at Vishwakarma publishing house, for production of this book. The last but not the least, I would record my sincere gratitude to the faculty, and the students at MIT School of Business, Pune for providing learning atmosphere that propelled me to write this book. I would fail in my duty if I do not thank all those unknown genius personalities who had designed many of these puzzles that I learnt since my childhood.

I would appreciate any comments or suggestions from the readers for improvement and additions to the book and would make endeavor to incorporate them in subsequent editions/ books.

Group Captain D. P. Apte (Retd.)
Director
MIT School of Business, Pune

FOREWORD

Since childhood, logic is an integral part of our behavior. When a child wants to abstain from the school, he gives an excuse of having a headache or a stomach ache. He does not claim having fever or cold or cough. Why? He knows that his mother cannot verify a headache but can immediately check fever or cold. He has thought logically in this case in order to push his agenda of not attending school.

Since ancient times, the word 'logic' has been associated with philosophy and this is enunciated by great literary works of saints and philosophers all over the world. They have extensively used logic in their various verses and commentaries in order to establish an easy and credible dialogue with their followers and the public in general. Each work of these great saints is a treasure trove of life's philosophy put logically.

'Logic' is the science of reasoning. 'Logic' is an important subject in itself. There are volumes written on the subject. But this is not the focus of the book that you are now reading. Here, the author has invited us to indulge in applying logic to solve some very simple and not so simple but interesting riddles and puzzles. These puzzles provide food for the brain and help to keep it sharp and active. They are also an ideal way to invest your time, whether individually or in a group.

Today we find an increasing number of people with neurological problems like Alzheimer's and dementia. Studies have proved that if the brain is properly exercised, it helps in keeping away from these distressful conditions. Solving crosswords, Sudoku and similar logical puzzles provide the required exercise to the brain to keep it sharp and active.

Algorithms are an integral part of the IT industry and logic is required in algorithms. Since the IT companies offer some of the most lucrative job opportunities today, it is imperative that the prospective employees, particularly the developers, be proficient in the subject. Therefore, several, if not most, of companies use 'aptitude test' and interviews as one of the tools in selection process for managerial and IT professional jobs. These tests primarily judge the analytical ability of a candidate. Logical riddles and puzzles form an important component of these tests. This book, therefore, also qualifies itself to be an important part of preparation for these selection processes. Sound logic is also useful for students preparing for CAT and similar competitive exams. This enhances the importance of this book for the students aspiring to be more competitive in such selection processes.

Considering all of the above, I sincerely feel that this book is the need of the hour. It is written in a very simple language, the puzzles are well illustrated, they come in varying degrees of difficulty, they cater to all age groups and all occupational groups and they have solutions given at the part II, with proper explanation.

I have known the author Prof. (Gp. Capt.) D. P. Apte for a long time. He is an engineer by vocation and now a teacher by profession, after having served for a long period with great distinction in the Indian Air Force. He is a dedicated social activist and a counselor who has cured many people of their 'sensitive emotional issues' by employing the simple yet effective techniques of 'Hawaiian HUNA' and NLP (Neuro Linguistic Programming). Writing of this book has come naturally to him, as he keeps himself busy in searching for new avenues for developing and sharing new skills. I am sure that this book will help the community to have a positive approach towards life in general and their mental health in particular.

Today the young generation is obsessed with technological advances such as smart phones, gaming and social media. Hence there is a dire need to refocus their attention to this very important aspect of development. I would particularly like to urge the parents of young school and college-going children to solve as many riddles as possible themselves and then encourage their children to do so. In fact, I would like to urge them to sit with their children and help them solve the puzzles. Not only would they be honing the skills of their children but also spending some quality time with them, which somehow we seem to have forgotten these days.

I hope all of you will enjoy the book as much as I did.

- Dr. Vijay P. Bhatkar

ABOUT THE BOOK

Why this book? I too had this question in mind. This book is not just for entertainment or fun. Neither is it intended only to test your knowledge. Before I explain the purpose of this book let me tell you how the idea for writing this book was conceived by me. In fact I so strongly felt the need for writing this book that I left the work on another important book that I was working on and started writing this book like an obsessed person.

It happened like this. One day one of my students came to me with couple of staff members and teachers. They wanted me to solve one puzzle urgently. I could see the tensed expression on my student's face and anxiety on the face of staff and faculty members accompanying him. What had happened was that he had appeared for a campus placement selection test of a reputed company. He had cleared the aptitude test and two rounds of interviews, one at campus and one at company office. Final interview was conducted by the CEO. The CEO was impressed with this boy so much that he changed the profile and wanted to take this student as his executive assistant. At the end of the interview, he gave him a puzzle and told him to solve it and send him the answer through email by 11 am the following day. Only then would he be given appointment. The boy worked on it throughout the night but could not solve it. So he approached the placement staff and faculty members the next morning, who worked on it for some time. When they could not find the solution till 1030 a.m. someone suggested that they approach me. Since I have been teaching subjects like Probability, Combinatorics, Operations Research, Statistical Methods, and also written few books on these subject, they presumed that I would be the better choice to ask for help. After reading the puzzle I promised him to solve it. In any case I could guess that the CEO would have already selected the student and just wanted to test the student's initiative and perseverance. As it happened I solved the puzzle in a few minutes and told the student to email it and then meet me. The puzzle was logical in nature and did not require any numerical or verbal aptitude.

When he came back, during discussion, I realized that many interviewers ask logical puzzles or quizzes which students find it difficult to answer. He also mentioned that during a recent recruitment of management graduates by one of the leading banks, students were asked 13 logical puzzles and many students struggled to solve these puzzles. On the very next day, there was a guest lecture by a General Manager (HR) of a major corporate house. He asked one logical puzzle which no student could answer. This set the ball rolling in my mind.

A thorough analysis led me to the following conclusion. We train students for Aptitude Test, Group Discussion, Personal Interviews and work on Personality Development programs besides core subject knowledge. However, there is hardly any training to develop logical thinking. This need is particularly felt among students of Engineering, IT, Management, etc. I learnt from an engineer working in Microsoft that it is very common to ask few logical puzzles in an interview. The way candidates solves it, plays an important role in the selection. So I felt the urgent need for developing these skills among students particularly for the students of this generation fed on internet and video entertainment. During my childhood we were fed on puzzles, riddles, quizzes by our teachers, seniors, parents and relatives since there was no TV, Video or Internet for entertainment. That was our means of entertainment and passing time, especially during the hot afternoons of summer vacations. This probably helped our generation to develop logical, analytical and critical thinking. Now I hardly see children and students being asked puzzles, riddles or quizzes as an entertainment. This is one of the ill-effects of improved technology and is a worldwide phenomenon.

A recent book 'Rethinking the MBA, Business education at a crossroad' written DrSrikantDatar, Dean, HBS and others also identified eight unmet needs of MBA programs. One of the identified needs is 'Critical and analytical thinking'. Let us see what the book has said about it. "We want people who can take an unstructured problem or a structured problem they can deconstruct, and look at it in a completely different way. ... We want people who can look at the problem and see it differently from others." The book further says "But what is critical thinking? And how can it be taught? ... To think critically is to reason clearly. It focuses on the thinking and reasoning process that underlines analysis and inquiry." (Emphasis provided).

So I embarked on designing and collecting logical puzzles from all possible sources. Many of them are very old ones that I had solved when I was a kid. Few I designed to develop specific analytical thinking process. Others I picked up from various sources. However, my focus is not only on the giving the solutions to the puzzles but also highlighting the thinking process to solve these puzzles. Hence besides giving solutions, I have explained logical thinking behind the solutions so that one can use the logical thinking process to solve similar puzzles. When I used these puzzles to start my lectures it also developed interest among students and motivated them to develop analytical thinking. I sincerely hope that, through this book, I would be successful in my endeavour to challenge, motivate and develop interest of the students on critical thinking and reasoning process. This would also improve students' reasoning and argument building skills. To my pleasant surprise, a couple of puzzles out of my collection were recently asked in an interview to my daughter who is IT professional.

Although I have started/published this book with a modest collection of 130 plus puzzles, I appeal to the readers that if they know some more logical puzzles, please share them with me so that I can include them in next edition. I have classified the puzzles in three levels of difficulty. I expect most readers to solve the Level 1 puzzles. Level 2 are relatively more difficult ones that many should be able to solve with some efforts. Don't get disheartened if you are unable to solve the Level 3 puzzles as they are quite difficult. I would like to exhort you not to jump to see the answers unless you work on them for a day or two. One of my faculty suggested to me that we print puzzles and answers as two separate parts. So parents could give puzzles to the children and keep the answers with them. This would resist the urge in children to see answers immediately. I thought that was a good idea so as to achieve the objective of the book to develop critical thinking and reasoning process for the children and students.

I feel that this book would be interesting reading for people of all ages, senior school children, college students, working professionals, housewives, and retired people. For some it is learning, for others entertainment, for yet others amusement!! I am sure that it would be an enriching experience to the readers. So enjoy the puzzles!!

Part 1

PUZZLES

To derive full benefit, do not refer to the answer unless you make enough efforts to solve the puzzle.

LOGIRIDDLES

To derive full benefit, do not refer to the answer unless you make enough efforts to solve the puzzle.

LOGIRIDDLES

1. There are eight balls. Out of these, seven are of identical weight and one defective ball is known to be heavy. Find out the heavy ball in maximum of two weighting using balance. (No weights are provided). **(Level 1)**

   Note: Same problem can have nine balls with one defective.

2. You have 26 constants, labeled A through Z. Let A equal 1. The other constants have values equal to the letter's position in the alphabet, raised to the power of the previous constant. That means that B (the second letter) = 2^A = 2^1 = 2. C = 3^B = 3^2 = 9, and so on. (* means multiplication and ^ means power)

   Find the exact numerical value for this expression: (X-A) * (X-B) * (X-C) * ... * (X-Y) * (X-Z) **(Level 1)**

3. There are eight balls. Of these, seven are of identical weight and one defective is heavy or light. You are given a balance without standard weights. Find out the defective in three weightings. **(Level 2)**

4. You have someone working for you for seven days and you have one gold bar to pay him. You must give him a one seventh piece of gold at the end of every day. At the end of the seventh day you will finish your gold bar. If you are allowed to make only two breaks in the gold bar, how do you pay your worker? **(Level 2)**

5. There are nine balls. Of these, eight are of identical weight and one is defective with different weight. Find out in three weightings, the defective ball and also whether it is heavy or light. **(Level 3)**

6. Kunal and Sourabh were excitedly describing the result of the Triangular cricket series. There were three contestants, Sri Lanka, Pakistan, and India. Kunal reported that Sri Lanka won the tournament, while Pakistan came second. Sourabh, on the other hand, reported that Indian won

To derive full benefit, do not refer to the answer unless you make enough efforts to solve the puzzle.

the tournament, while Sri Lanka came second. In fact, neither Kunal nor Sourabh had given a correct report of the results of the triangular series. Each of them had given one correct statement and one false statement. What was the actual placing of the three contestants? **(Level 1)**

7. There are four people who need to walk across a bridge in the middle of the night to get to the other side. The bridge is only wide and strong enough for two people to cross at a time. They have only one flashlight which they must use while crossing the bridge. When two people cross, they must cross at the slower member's speed. Because it is a night, while crossing alone or as a pair, they must have a flashlight. All four people must cross the bridge and have all four on the other side of the bridge in 17 minutes, since the bridge will collapse in exactly that amount of time. Here are the times each member takes to cross the bridge:

   Person A: 1 minute,   Person B: 2 minutes,
   Person C: 5 minutes,   Person D: 10 minutes

   How can all four people get across the bridge within 17 minutes? **(Level 3)**

   Note: You cannot do tricky stuff like throwing the flashlight, etc.

8. At a family reunion were the following people: one grandfather, one grandmother, two fathers, two mothers, four children, three grandchildren, one brother, two sisters, two sons, two daughters, one father-in-law, one mother-in-law, and one daughter-in-law. But not as many people attended as it sounds. How many were there, and who were they? **(Level 1)**

9. 97 baseball teams participate in a tournament. The champion is chosen for this tournament by the usual elimination scheme. That is, the 97 teams are divided into pairs, and the two teams of each pair play against each other. The loser of each pair is eliminated, and the remaining teams are paired up again, etc. How

many games must be played to determine a champion?
(Level 2)

10. Your sock drawer contains ten pairs of white socks and ten pairs of black socks. If you're only allowed to take one sock from the drawer at a time and you can't see what color sock you're taking until you've taken it, how many socks do you have to take before you're guaranteed to have at least one matching pair? **(Level 1)**

11. Two days ago, Neha was 8 years old. Next year, she'll be 11 years old. How is this possible? **(Level 2)**

12. A man is the owner of a winery who recently passed away. In his will, he left 21 barrels (seven of which are filled with wine, seven of which are half full, and seven of which are empty) to his three sons. However, the wine and barrels must be split so that each son has the same number of full barrels, the same number of half-full barrels, and the same number of empty barrels. Note that there are no measuring devices handy. How can the barrels and wine be evenly divided? **(Level 1)**

13. Facts:

   A: There are 5 houses in 5 different colors.
   B: In each house lives a person with a different nationality.
   C: These 5 owners drink a certain beverage, smoke a certain brand of cigar and keep a certain pet.
   D: No owner has the same pet, smoke the same brand of cigar or drink the same drink.

   Hints given:

   1: The British lives in a red house.
   2: The Swede keeps dogs as pets.
   3: The Dane drinks tea.
   4: The green house is on the left of the white house (it also means they are next door to each other).
   5: The green house owner drinks coffee.

   _{To derive full benefit, do not refer to the answer unless you make enough efforts to solve the puzzle.}

LOGIRIDDLES

6: The person who smokes Pall Mall rears birds.
7: The owner of the yellow house smokes Dunhill.
8: The man living in the house right in the center drinks milk.
9: The Norwegian lives in the first house.
10: The man who smokes Blend lives next to the one who keeps cats.
11: The man who keeps horses lives next to the man who smokes Dunhill.
12: The owner who smokes Blue Master drinks beer.
13: The German smokes Prince.
14: The Norwegian lives next to the blue house.
15: The man who smokes Blend has a neighbor who drinks water.

The question is: who keeps the fish? **(Level 3)**

14. A mountain goat attempts to scale a cliff sixty feet high. Every minute, the goat climbs three feet but then slips back two feet. How long does it take for the goat to reach the top? **(Level 1)**

15. You are a prisoner sentenced to death. The Emperor offers you a chance to live by playing a simple game. He gives you 50 black marbles, 50 white marbles and 2 empty bowls. He then says, "Divide these 100 marbles into these 2 bowls. You can divide them any way you like as long as you use all the marbles. Then I will blindfold you and shuffle the bowls around. You then can choose one bowl and remove ONE marble. If the marble is WHITE you will live, but if the marble is BLACK... you will die." How do you divide the marbles up so that you have the greatest probability of choosing a WHITE marble? **(Level 3)**

16. Ship has a ladder hanging with 10 steps below water level and 30 steps above water level. Each step of the ladder is of 1 foot height. During high tide, water level rises at the rate of three feet per hour. During low tide, water level drops by two feet per hour. How many steps would be

below water after three hours of high tide followed by two hours of low tide? **(Level 1)**

17. 500 men are arranged in an array of 10 rows and 50 columns. Tallest among each row of all are asked to come out. And the shortest among them is A. Similarly after resuming them to their original positions, the shortest among each column are asked to come out. And the tallest among them is B. Now who is taller A or B? **(Level 2)**

18. You have a tank of milk with a tap. You have two measures one with 5 liter capacity and one with 3 liter capacity. You need to deliver 4 liters milk to a customer along with the container. The customer does not have any container. How will you do it? What is the minimum number of steps required? **(Level 2)**

19. There are 20 mathematicians assembled in a hall for conference. They are known to be very intelligent. The queen of that country wants to test whether they are really most intelligent in the world. So she announces that the next day is her birth day and she wants to definitely invite few of them for party in her castle.

Her method of inviting is somewhat different. She puts condition that they all have to sleep in the night in the same hall. When they all are asleep, a knight from the castle would come to the hall and put a red mark (bindi) on the forehead of all who are invited. Next day when they get up all those who have a mark on their forehead must attend party at castle and those who do not have a mark are not to attend the party. If anyone without a mark on the forehead comes to castle, will be put in jail. She also says that if the person who has a mark on forehead does not come to the castle will be considered as her personal insult and that person will be send to gallows. She also puts the condition that no one will talk to any other person or communicate with any other way except looking and observing at each other. She also puts the condition that none of them is allowed to see their reflection in mirror or water or in each other's eyes or any other way. Then she announces that there will be shuttle service of horse coaches with adequate capacity and as many times as required from morning to evening. Those who want to come to the castle can use them whenever they feel like. She also says that if the right people come for the party all will be awarded with gold coins.

Next day morning all the mathematicians get up look at each other and think. They are all very intelligent. All invited correctly manage to go for the party and others stay back. All are then rewarded by the queen. How did they manage to go for the party correctly? **(Level 3)**

20. There are 20 married couples at a party. Each person shakes hands with every person other than her or his spouse. Find the total number of handshakes. **(Level 1)**

21. You have a tank of milk with a tap. You have two measures one with 5 liter capacity and one with 3 liter capacity. You need to deliver 4 liters milk to a customer. The customer has a container. Once taken out you can not put the milk back in the tank and of course you won't like to throw any milk also. How will you do it? What is the minimum number of steps required? **(Level 2)**

22. In how many ways can four small size squares, not all in the same column or row, be selected from 8 X 8 chess board to form a rectangle? **(Level 1)**

23. One adventurer enters the cave and gets trapped. He has very limited 7 days stock of food and water. From the point where he is now there are three paths. One would take him out of the cave after walking for one day. Other two paths are connected to each other with total walking distance of three days. The adventure have flash light that could last for seven days. Entries of all the three paths look identical.

a) What are the chances that adventurer will survive if every time after coming back to the original point he starts again? What is the expected number of days he would come out?

b) What are the chances that adventurer will survive if every time after coming back to the original point he avoids the path that he has just come? What is the expected number of days he would come out?

c) What are the chances that adventurer will survive if he has a marker pen? What would be the expected number of days he would come out?   **(Level 3)**

24. A company has manufactured steel balls of 10gm weight each in fifty batches. Suppose one of the batches is defective and has weight of each ball more (or less) by 0.2 gm than the required standard of 10 gm. However we don't know which batch is defective. You have an electronic weighing machine that can find a weight up to milligrams. Find in one weighing which batch is defective? **(Level 2)**

25. Ten cards are drawn from a pack of 52 with replacement. How many ways it can be drawn if 10th card is the first to be repeated?   **(Level 1)**

26. Prove that palindrome of even length is divisible by 11.
     (Level 3)

27. Given a '8 X 8' chess board.
   i)   How many squares of all sizes are there on it?
   ii) How many rectangles of all sizes are there on it?
     (Level 1)

28. How many ways are there to place two identical rooks in a common row or column on an '8 X 8' chess board?
     (Level 2)

29. How many ways are there to place 2 identical queens on an 8 X 8 chess board, so that they are not placed in common row or column or diagonal?   **(Level 2)**

To derive full benefit, do not refer to the answer unless you make enough efforts to solve the puzzle.

30. In how many ways can two small size squares be selected from 8 X 8 chess board so that they are not in the same row or same column? **(Level 2)**

31. In how many ways can four small size squares, not all in the same column or row, be selected from 8 X 8 chess board? **(Level 1)**

32. In how many different ways two adjacent squares can be selected from 8 X 8 chessboard, if
    a) Squares are of smallest size?
    b) Squares are of any size? **(Level 2)**

33. Find the number of ways of factoring 441000 in two factors m and n which are relatively prime. (i.e. there are no common factors other than 1 between m and n) **(Level 2)**

34. A year is a leap year if it is (i) either a multiple of 4 but not of 100, or (ii) a multiple of 400. Find the number of leap years between, a) 1000 and 3000 both inclusive. b) 1884 and 4004 both inclusive. **(Level 1)**

35. A man has 6 friends. At dinner in a certain restaurant, he has met each of them 12 times, every two of them 6 times, every three of them 4 times every four of them 3 times, every five of them twice and all of them only once. He has dined out without meeting any of them 8 times. How many times has he dined out altogether? **(Level 2)**

36. How many students must be in a class to guarantee that at least two students receive the same score, if exam is graded on a scale 0 to 100 points? **(Level 1)**

37. During a month with 30 days, a team plays at least one game a day, but no more than 45 games. Show that there must be a period of some number of consecutive days during which the team must play exactly 14 games. **(Level 3)**

38. There are six people in a group. Each pair of individuals consists of two friends or two enemies. Show that there are either three mutual friends or three mutual enemies in the group. **(Level 3)**

39. What is the minimum number of people so that at least two of them will have their birthday on the same day of the week? **(Level 1)**

40. Show that given any set of seven integers, there must exist, two integers in this set whose sum or difference is divisible by 10. **(Level 2)**

41. Show that in any group there will be at least two people who know the same number of people in the group.
    (Level 3)

42. Consider a tournament in which n players play against every other player. If each player wins at least one match, show that there are at least two players having the same number of wins. **(Level 3)**

43. A man has a wolf, a goat, and a grass. He must cross a river with the two animals and the grass. There is a small rowing-boat, in which he can take only one thing with him at a time. If, however, the wolf and the goat are left alone, the wolf will eat the goat. If the goat and the grass are left alone, the goat will eat the grass. How can the man get across the river with the two animals and the grass?
    (Level 1)

44. Show that at a party of 20 people, there are two who have same number of friends. **(Level 3)**

45. Among the integers 1,2,....., 200, if any 101 integers are chosen then show that there are two among these such that one is divisible by other. **(Level 3)**

46. MLA hostel has 90 rooms, however there are 100 MLAs. Keys are to be issued to all the MLAs, so that any 90 MLAs can have access to one room each. Find What is

To derive full benefit, do not refer to the answer unless you make enough efforts to solve the puzzle.

minimum number of keys required, and how these to be distributed? **(Level 2)**

47. There are 51 houses on a street. Each house has an address between 1000 and 1099 both inclusive. Show that at least two houses have addresses that are consecutive integers. **(Level 3)**

48. Highway department wants to check a traffic density of a junction. To automate the process it puts sensors that measure number of vehicles crossing the junction point per minute. To identity the type of vehicles as two wheelers, three-wheelers (auto rickshaws) and four wheelers it puts pressure sensor array on the road that finds out number of wheels that have crossed the junction point. In five minutes the sensors record 250 vehicles and 615 wheels having crossed the junction. We know that the auto rickshaws are regulated to run maximum of one per minute on the road leading to the junction. How many two wheelers, three wheelers and four wheelers passed through the junction in five minutes? **(Level 2)**

49. There was a young man sailing in a ship. In the middle of the ocean his ship capsized. All on the ship drowned while only few survived by floating on a life boat. They reached one island, but unfortunately captured by cannibals inhabited on the island. When taken to the king of cannibals, they pleaded for mercy and one chance. The king finally said, "You are lucky to have survived in the ocean infested by sharks. So, it's not fair for me to kill you without giving chance. You can make any statement. I will decide whether it is true or false. My decision is final. If your statement is 'True', we will cut you in to pieces and eat you raw. If your statement is 'False' we will roast you and eat you." The king also said, "If you survive, I will give you a boat. You can use the boat to go to other island where ships come regularly. So you could be free and go to your home."

To derive full benefit, do not refer to the answer unless you make enough efforts to solve the puzzle.

Then he separates the survivors and takes them in jungle one by one. All get killed except the confident young man. He was let go with a boat. He became free. What was the statement he made to the king? **(Level 3)**

50. If the average of n positive numbers is t, then show that,
    a) At least one of the numbers is greater than or equal to t.
    b) Further at least one of them is less than or equal to t.
    (Level 1)

51. There were prisoners sentenced to life in a jail. The jail had two layers of walls. You need to go out from the door of the first layer walk 100 meters and then go out from a door. It had two doors to the first and second layer. On the occasion of the birth of a prince, a hair to the throne, king decides to mitigate some punishment of prisoners. So he visits the prison and tells prisoners that there are two gates to the inner wall. One is manned by a guard who always tells lie whereas the other gate has a guard who always tells the truth. But the king does not tell who is at which gate. One gate takes them to freedom whereas one gate takes them to gallows. He tells prisoners that they can walk one at a time to any one of the gate, ask any question that can be answered only as 'Yes' / 'No' or 'True' / 'False'. Then the prisoner can decide which gate to use and go out from any gate. He also gives a choice to stay where they are and continue with the life term. Most of the prisoners decide to stay on and continue their life term. Few want to try their luck. After all, their chances are 50:50. But the risks are very high. Going from wrong door means death.

    One intelligent prisoner was smiling. When asked by the king, he says "I am certain that I will be free." When his turn comes he asks one question & then decides the gate and walks out to freedom. King with curiosity asks him "How were you so confident? What was your question?" So, what was the question he asked to the guard? **(Level 3)**

    _{To derive full benefit, do not refer to the answer unless you make enough efforts to solve the puzzle.}

52. Three friends Sourabh, Shirish, and Pushkar are talking to each other about the number of 'Hummers' with Sachin Tendulkar. Sourabh says: "There are at least four 'Hummers' with Sachin Tendulkar." Shirish says: "No, there are less than four 'Hummers' with Sachin Tendulkar." "According me," says Pushkar, "There is at least one 'Hummers' with Sachin Tendulkar." If you know that only one of the three friends is right, how many 'Hummers' are there with Sachin Tendulkar? **(Level 1)**

53. In the middle of a round pool lays a beautiful water-lily. The water-lily doubles in size every day. After exactly 20 days the complete pool will be covered by the lily. After how many days will half of the pool be covered by the water-lily? **(Level 1)**

54. The following four cards sit on a table:

    A B 6 9

    Each card has a digit on one side and a letter on the other side. Which cards should you turn around to test the following statement: "when there is a vowel on one side of a card, then there is an even digit on the other side"? **(Level 2)**

55. Parag has one of the numbers 1, 2, or 3 in mind. Sheetal is allowed to ask one question to Parag to find out which of these three numbers he has in mind. Parag will answer this question only with the answers "yes", "no", or "I can't say". Which question should Sheetal ask Parag to find out in one time which number he has in mind? **(Level 3)**

56. A light bulb is hanging in a room. Outside of the room there are three switches, of which only one is connected to the lamp. In the starting situation, all switches are 'off' and the bulb is not lit. You cannot see the bulb or its light from outside. You can operate any of the switches from outside and then go only once in to the room to check the bulb. How can you determine which of the three switches is connected to the light bulb? **(Level 2)**

57. A rather silly car thief stole a car of the chief of police. Obviously he did not know it, otherwise he would not have stolen it and created problem for himself. The police immediately started an investigation and arrested four suspects who were seen near the car at the time of the crime. Chief of police asked the police station in-charge to examine the suspects using the lie-detector available at the police HQ. Each suspect gave three statements during the examinations. These are listed below:

Suspect A: 1) In high-school I was in the same class as suspect C. 2) Suspect B has no driving license. 3) The thief didn't know that it was the car of the chief of police.

Suspect B: 1) Suspect C is the guilty one. 2) Suspect A is not guilty. 3) I never sat behind the wheel of a car.

Suspect C: 1) I never met suspect A until today. 2) Suspect B is innocent. 3) Suspect D is the guilty one.

Suspect D: 1) Suspect C is innocent. 2) I didn't do it. 3) Suspect A is the guilty one.

After returning from police HQ the police station in-charge got confused and with so many contradicting statements, lost track. He only remembered that the lie-detector had reported that exactly four of the twelve statements were true, and remaining statements were false. But he did not remember which ones were true and which ones false. But he did not want to tell chief to carryout the lie-detector test again. So he decided to use his logical skills. Finally he does find the car chief. Who is the car thief? **(Level 3)**

58. Four gentlemen (Deepak, Prasanna, Parag, and Nachiket) went to an expensive restaurant to dine. They checked their coats, hats, gloves, and canes at the door (each of the gentlemen had one of each). But when they checked out, there was a mix up, and each of the men ended up with exactly one article of clothing (a pair of gloves is considered a single article of clothing) belonging to each

To derive full benefit, do not refer to the answer unless you make enough efforts to solve the puzzle.

one of the four. Deepak and Prasanna ended up with their own coats, Parag ended up with his own hat, and Nachiket ended up with his own gloves. Deepak did not end up with Parag's cane. State whose coat, hat, gloves, and cane each of the gentlemen ended up with. **(Level 2)**

59. Yesterday evening, Pournima and her husband invited their relatives (two couples) for a dinner at home. The six of them sat at a round table. Pournima tells you the following:
    a) "Prasanna, a man, sat on the left of the woman who sat on the left of the man who sat on the left of Pranita who is a woman.
    b) Sheetal who is a woman sat on the left of the man who sat on the left of the woman who sat on the left of the man who sat on the left of the woman who sat on the left of my husband.
    c) Parag who is a man sat on the left of the woman who sat on the left of Deepak who is a man.
    d) I did not sit beside my husband."

    What is the name of Pournima's husband?   **(Level 2)**

60. Suhas and his wife went to a party where four other married couples were present. Every person shook hands with everyone he or she was not acquainted with. When the handshaking was over, Suhas asked everyone, including his wife, how many hands they shook. To his surprise, he got nine different answers. How many hands did Suhas's wife shake?   **(Level 3)**

61. There are three boxes with fruits: one box with apples, one box with mangos, and one box with both apples and mangos. The boxes have labels that describe the contents, but none of these labels is on the right box. How can you determine what each of the boxes contains, by taking only one piece of fruit from only one box?   **(Level 2)**

62. Is it possible to cut the chess-board into pieces (over the lines!) such that each piece has twice as many squares of

one color than that of the other color (i.e. twice as many black squares as white squares or twice as much white squares as black squares)? Give a proof! **(Level 3)**

63. Santa Singh is a strange liar. He lies on six days of the week, but on the seventh day he always tells the truth. He made the following statements on three successive days:

Day 1: "I lie on Monday and Tuesday."
Day 2: "Today, it's Thursday, Saturday, or Sunday."
Day 3: "I lie on Wednesday and Friday."

On which day does Santa Singh tell the truth? **(Level 3)**

64. You have a chess board (8x8) with two squares from diagonally opposite corners are removed. You want to fill the chess board with bricks of size 2 small squares of chess board oriented vertically or horizontally. No overlaps, no gaps, and no bricks crossing the borders are permitted. Is this possible? (Give Proof) **(Level 1)**

65. Three Police officers were taking three prisoners from one place to other through thick jungle. They come across a river that had to be crossed. There was only one motor boat that can take only two people across at a time. All the police officers had radio compass which is a must if one has to survive through the jungle and reach a habitation. Otherwise in the jungle death is certain. Hence it is in the interest of the prisoners not to run away unless they overpower the police officers and take radio compass. Every Police officer is trained and capable of handling one prisoner. However, if there are more prisoners than the police officers on any one place (bank) at any time, prisoners will overpower the police officers and run away. All the police officers can operate the boat. On the other hand only one prisoner knows how to operate the boat. Since the river is infested with crocodiles there no possibility of any prisoner jumping in the river from the boat and escaping. The task of the police officers is to take prisoners across. Can prisoners be taken across by police officers? How? **(Level 2)**

<small>To derive full benefit, do not refer to the answer unless you make enough efforts to solve the puzzle.</small>

66. You have two glasses of 200 ml, one half filled (100 ml) with alcohol and one half filled (100ml) with water. 10 ml of the alcohol is taken and added to the glass containing water. The mixture is stirred. Then 10 ml of this mixture is mixed back into the alcohol. This process is repeated once more. Now is there more alcohol in the original glass of water or more water in the original glass of alcohol? **(Level 1)**

67. The professor Patwardhan, Haridas, Limaye, and Vamburkar are all teachers at the same business school. Each Professor teaches two different subjects. We also know following facts:

a) Three Professors teach Finance
b) There is only one math Professor
c) There are two teachers for Law
d) Two Professors, Meghana and Haridas, teach Economics
e) Professor Umesh doesn't teach Finance
f) Professor Anjali is Law teacher
g) Professor Patwardhan doesn't teach any course that is taught by Professor Shailashree or Professor Limaye.

What is the full name of each Professor and which two subjects does each one teach? **(Level 2)**

68. Sourabh and Poorwa played a game of Cross and Naught. In this game, two players makes a move alternately in turns with one player putting Cross and other player putting Naught (X or O) in a 3X3 grid. The players try to get three circles or three crosses in a row (horizontal, vertical, or diagonal). Whosoever completes the three circles or three crosses in a row or column or diagonally first wins. Both Sourabh and Poorwa are intelligent and wanted to win. So they always tried to put X or O such that whenever possible they must win and otherwise they tried to block opponent from winning. Both would not miss any chance to put X or O as and when they could complete the row with their symbol during their turn.

They together made six moves and had to leave the game. So Sourabh asked his father Deepak to continue on his behalf with symbol X and Poorwa asked her Mother Sandhya to continue for her with symbol O. Then they both left with game position as below:

O	O	
O	X	
X	X	

However, Sourabh and Poorwa forgot to tell whose turn it is or who started the game. Sandhya asks Deepak how can we continue and decide who will win this game? Deepak replies don't worry I will tell you. So who wins the game? **(Level 2)**

69. Given below is a small railway shunting-yard with two wagons A and B positioned on the rail segment 1 and 2. There is a locomotive (engine) on the rail segment 3. The wagons are of 5 meter length, and the locomotive is of 10 meter length. Segments 1 and 2 are merged and continue for long distance. Segments 1 and 3 merge with the dead end up to the buffer-stop. The switch on the dead end of joined segments of 1 and 3 has a length of 5 meters. So the locomotive cannot change tracks on the merged joint of 1 and 3. The dead end between the switch and the buffer-stop on the junction of segments 2 and 3 has a length of 15 meters. The locomotive can move forward and backward, and can both pull and push wagons.

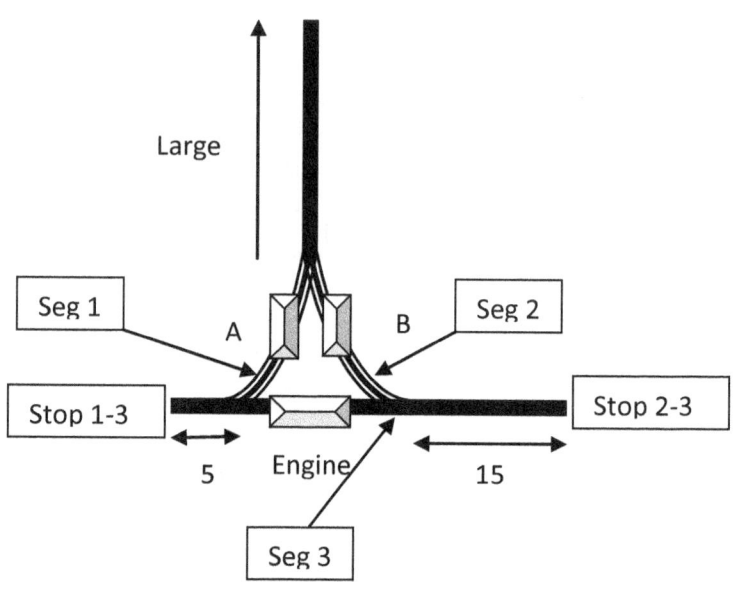

How must the locomotive shunt the wagons, to arrive in a situation where the wagons have changed places and the locomotive is back in its starting position? **(Level 3)**

70. A company has manufactured steel balls of 10 gm weight each in eight batches. Suppose two of the batches are defective and has weight of each ball in that batch 10.2 gm (0.2 gm more than required standard). However we don't know which batch is defective. You have an electronic weighing machine that can find a weight up to milligrams. Find in one weighing which batch is defective? **(Level 2)**

71. There are total 8 people who want to cross a river there is a boat on which only two persons can travel at a time. Out of 8 people; 1 is a policeman, 1 is thief, 4 children(2 boys and 2 girls), husband and wife (father and mother of all 4 children). The thief can't stay alone with family members without the policeman. Boys can't stay with mother if father is not there. Girls can't stay with father if mother is not there. Only policeman, husband and wife can row the boat. Find how they can cross the river. **(Level 3)**

72. One intelligent man was travelling riding on a horse. He saw three men quarreling. When he asked them the

reason, came to know that they were three brothers. Their father died leaving 19 horses. In his will, father has stated that half of the horses are to be given to the elder brother, quarter of the horses to the younger brother and one fifth to the youngest brother. The brothers said, "We thought that our father was wise. But now it appears that he was a bit cranky. Otherwise how could he make a will that requires us to cut the horses? Now our problem is how will we cut the horses and which way will we distribute. No one wants to compromise and reduce his share." The intelligent man thought for a while, smiled and completed the distribution of horses. When he left on his horse, all the brothers were happy and wondered their father was indeed very clever. How were the horses distributed? **(Level 2)**

73. Army unit commander wants to send a secret plan to a field officer. He has a box which can be fitted with four locks, and has several locks and their corresponding keys. However, the field officer does not have any keys to your locks. If commander sends a key separately, he suspects that the key could be copied en route and misused. How can he ensure the secret plan is delivered securely to the officer? **(Level 2)**

74. There was a farmer who had a beautiful young daughter. The farmer in his bad times had borrowed money from an old ugly moneylender. When the farmer was unable to pay back the loan and asked for some more time, the money lender refused and came to acquire his land and evict the farmer. All villagers pleaded to the money lender to give the farmer more time to pay back. Money lender looked at the farmer's daughter and told the villagers, that he will waive the loan if farmer's daughter marries him. This was of course objected by the farmer and his daughter. When the villagers ask money lender to give some concession, money lender says, "I will give the daughter on chance. I will put two small pebbles, one white and one black in a cloth bag. The girl then has to pick one of the pebbles

blindfolded. If the pebble picked is black, she has to marry me. If it is white I will waive the entire loan." The girl decides to sacrifice and accept the condition. Father was very sad. The girl thought her chance is 50-50. In any case her father would be out of the debt. Then the money lender picks up two pebbles. But the girl and father notice that the money lender had cunningly taken both black pebbles and put in the bag. However, they had to keep quite as villagers would not have listen complaint against the money lender. So the father tells his daughter to withdraw from the condition and handover his land. But daughter is firm. She was known to be very intelligent. She finds the way out. What did she do to come out of the situation victorious? **(Level 2)**

75. You have a refrigerator with a freezer compartment capable of holding seven ice cube trays stacked vertically. But there are no shelves to separate the trays, and if you stack one tray on top of another before the ice cubes in the bottom tray are fully frozen, the top tray will nestle into it, and you won't get full cubes in the bottom tray. You have enough trays, each of which can make a dozen cubes. It takes 10 minutes to freeze water in the tray in to ice. In 30 minutes you expect guests to arrive. How many maximum number of full-sized ice cubes you can make before guests arrive? **(Level 3)**

76. A man is looking at a photograph of someone. His friend asks who it is. The man replies, "Brothers and sisters, I have none. But that man's father is my father's son." Who was in the photograph? **(Level 1)**

77. Why is it better to have round manhole covers than square ones? **(Level 2)**

78. Four switches are outside a closed room and can be turned on or off. One is the light switch for the incandescent overhead light in the next room but you don't know which. The other three switches do nothing that you can notice. When you reach all the switches are off. From outside the

room with the switches in it, you can't see whether the light in the next room is turned on or off. The door has hydraulic closer. You may flip the switches as often and as many times as you like, but once you enter the next room to check on the light, you must be able to say which switch controls the light without flipping the switches any further. (And you can't open the door without entering, either!) How can you determine which switch controls the light? **(Level 3)**

79. An old Arab was worried that his ancestral house would be split by his two feuding sons. So he wanted to give it only to one son. He did not want to be partial so he makes a proposition. His two sons will ride their own camels in a race, and whichever camel crosses the finish line last will win the property. Before he could witness the race he died. The people from the village insisted that the wish of the old man must be fulfilled for deciding the ownership of the property. The race was arranged. During the race, the two brothers wander aimlessly for days, neither willing to cross the finish line. Villagers were fed up. So the two sons were tired too but did not want to give up without fight. In desperation, villagers ask a wise man for advice. He came and called both sons. Then he told something in the ears of the two sons. Suddenly the villagers saw both the brothers leapt onto the camels and charge toward the finish line. Thus the race was over quickly. What did the wise man say? **(Level 2)**

80. There was a pent-angular 20-20 cricket tournament. Sourabh gave clues to Parag as to how the five teams finished -- which may have included some ties. Determine how the five teams finished based on the following clues:
    a) Pakistan finished above Australia and below India.
    b) India tied with Pakistan if and only if South Africa did not tie with Sri Lanka.
    c) Pakistan finished as many places below Sri Lanka as Sri Lanka finished below India if and only if India finished above Australia.

To derive full benefit, do not refer to the answer unless you make enough efforts to solve the puzzle.

Parag thought for a moment, and then answered correctly. How did the five teams finish the tournament? **(Level 1)**

81. Three surgeons were travelling through a jungle in a car with a driver. The car meets with a major accident where all the three surgeons get bruises on their right hands. Unfortunately the driver's injuries were serious and needed surgery. They had the equipment necessary for the driver's surgery with them, and they can use the campfire to sterilize the tools. But there are only two rubber gloves. Because of the different surgeons' skills, all three of the surgeons are needed to operate on the driver, in sequence. All of them have to use right hand for the surgery. However all of them are worried for exposing open wounds to other's blood and possibility of getting infection through blood. There is no water to wash the gloves also. How can this be done without any of them being exposed to the blood of any of the others? **(Level 3)**

82. Three friends went to a hotel and had snacks. They had decided to equally share the bill. When the bill was produced of Rs 250, all of them put Rs 100 notes each in the tray and gave it to the waiter. The waiter brought Rs 50. The friends paid Rs 20 as a tip and took Rs 10 each and left. Later, the waiter got confused. He told to his friend that the friends had Rs 300 when they came. They spend Rs 90 each totaling Rs 270. He got Rs 20 as tip from them. That makes total expenditure of Rs 290. Where did the remaining Rs 10 go? Where did it vanish? Can you help him to find it? **(Level 2)**

83. You have a 12 liter jug, an 8 liter jug, and a 5 liter jug. None of the jugs have any markings on them. The 12 liter jug is full, and the other two are empty. How can you divide the 12 liters of water equally (i.e., so two of the jugs have exactly 6 liters of water in them, and the third is empty)? **(Level 1)**

84. You are on a game show. You are shown three closed doors. A prize is hidden behind one, and the game show

To derive full benefit, do not refer to the answer unless you make enough efforts to solve the puzzle.

host knows where it is. You are asked to select a door. You do. Before you open it, the host opens one of the other doors, showing that it is empty, and then asks you if you'd like to change your guess. Should you or should you not, or doesn't it matter? **(Level 3)**

85. One day a girl celebrated her birthday. Two days later, her older twin brother celebrated his. How is this possible? **(Level 1)**

86. You and your spouse go on an organized tour with four other couples. During introduction, it is discovered that, each person except you were acquainted (known to each other) a different number of the people prior to the tour. How many people did your spouse know prior to the tour? How many people did you know prior to the tour? **(Level 3)**

87. All of my flowers except two are roses. All of my flowers except two are tulips. All of my flowers except two are carnations. How many flowers do I have? **(Level 1)**

88. A rotary contactor connects a control panel to seven systems through seven contact points arranged in a perfect circular arrangement. On one face of the rotary contactor have seven contact points where seven input signals are available that control seven systems. On the other corresponding surface of the contactors there are seven output points connected to seven systems. Only one system is required to work at a time. This is achieved by rotating the rotary contactor in steps of one seventh revolutions through computer control and then putting on the supply. Thus by rotating the connector, it can be connected to the outlet in any of seven different ways. Each of the connector point is numbered from one to seven, each number being used exactly once. The same is true for the contact points of the outlet. The device that uses this cable only requires that one of the connector contacts to match up to its corresponding output contacts in order to operate. How should you number the connector

To derive full benefit, do not refer to the answer unless you make enough efforts to solve the puzzle.

contacts on the input and output side so that, no matter how the contactor is rotated only one connector contact matches up? **(Level 3)**

89. Five couples went hiking. They encountered a river that was swift and deep. The only way to cross it was one boat. But it would only hold maximum of three people. Women were not comfortable to stay along with men if their husband is not present with them. Hence they refused to stay with other men unless their husband was with them. All the men and only one woman could operate the boat. How did the five couples cross the river? **(Level 2)**

90. On your travels, three men stand at a fork in the road. One road goes to town and other to jungle. You're not sure which fork you need to take to go to town, but each of the three men do. One of these people tells the truth, one always lies, and the third tells the truth sometimes and lies the other times. Each of the three men knows each of the others, but you don't know who is who. If you could ask only one of the men (chosen at random, since you don't know which man is which) one yes/no type question, what question would you ask to determine the road you wish to take? **(Level 3)**

91. Poorwa, Sourabh, and Neha started number of small businesses. They wanted to open different bank accounts for different businesses according to who are all involved in that business. Each of them opened one individual account for their own transactions. Each pair opened one joint account without taking the third person. One joint account was opened by all three. Of the Poorwa's accounts, two were in SBI. Of the Sourabh's accounts, three were in SBI. Of the Neha's accounts, four were in SBI. How many accounts were opened in SBI? How many accounts were opened in other banks? **(Level 1)**

92. A card-shuffling machine always rearranges cards in the same way relative to the original order of the cards.

All of the hearts, arranged in order from ace to king, were put into the machine. The cards were shuffled and then put into the machine again. After this second shuffling, the cards were in the following order: 10, 9, Q, 8, K, 3, 4, A, 5, J, 6, 2 and 7. What was the order after the first shuffle? **(Level 3)**

93. Four men A, B, C and D participating in a game were asked to stand one behind other with some distance. They were all facing the same direction such that A was at the back of the line, and D at the front. Between C and D partition was kept. So A, at the back of the line, could see B and C. B could see C. Neither of the C or D could see anybody. The participants were blind fold and put one hat each. They were told that two of them are wearing black hats and two of them white hats. They were given a challenge that they can win Rs 10000 if any one of them correctly recognizes the color of his own hat. The men are not allowed to talk amongst themselves. How will they ensure that one of them correctly recognizes colour of his hat? **(Level 2)**

94. Height of a plant and a boy was equal to 3 feet. A permanent mark was made at half of their heights. That is at a midpoint of tree height i.e. one and half feet from ground one nail was driven in. Similarly a mark was made with a permanent tattoo at one and half feet from the feet. A mark was also made on the hand at same level of the tattoo on the body. After 10 years the height of the boy doubles to 6 feet. At the same time the height of the tree increases to four times to 12 feet. What would be the approximate difference between the heights from the ground of the tattoo on the hand and nail mark on the tree? **(Level 1)**

95. This is very famous puzzle during my childhood. Can you completely trace the following figure without lifting your pen or tracing a line more than once? If yes how? If not, why not? **(Level 3)**

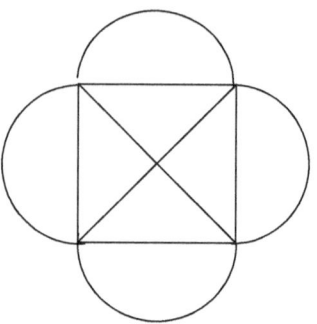

96. Sourabh has enough boxes in three sizes: large, standard, and small. He puts 15 large boxes on a table. He leaves some of these boxes empty, and in all the other boxes he puts 10 standard boxes each. He leaves some of these standard boxes empty, and in all the other standard boxes he puts 10 (empty) small boxes each. Now, 114 of all the boxes on the table are empty. How many boxes has Sourabh used in total? (Level 3)

97. In a TV game a team of five smart contestants was participating. Four team members were lined up so that each one can see the ones in front of him/her but not the ones behind. (The last one can see the other three, and the front one can't see anybody.) The fifth member who is captain is asked to stand outside and watch. They are told that there are total of four hats of three colours; red, white, and blue. They would be blind folded and one hat each will be placed on the heads of each team member. Then the blind fold would be removed. Each of the four hats are one of three different colours (red, white, and blue), and there is at least one hat of each colour. Each of the team members standing in a line in turns has to recognize the colour of the hat he/she is wearing and say it loudly so that other members could hear. The captain is asked to select any sequence of the hats but not to discuss it with the other team members or tell the team members about the sequence. What sequence of the hats he must suggest such that the team members can recognize the colour of the hats they are wearing without guessing. No one in the team including the captain knows which of the three

colours is used for two identical hats. What sequence did the captain recommend? **(Level 2)**

98. An old man wanted to hand over his business to one of his son who is clever. He had nine birds. He puts a condition to his sons that who could put these nine birds in four cages so that each cage has odd number of birds would get control of his business. One of the sons says to his father how is it possible? Sum of four odd numbers is always even. The other son smiles and could make four cages such that the nine birds are distributed in those cages such that each cage has an odd number of birds. How did he do it? **(Level 2)**

99. Of three men, one always tells the truth, one always tells lie and one answer "yes" or "no" randomly. Each man knows which one each of the others is. You may ask three yes/no questions, to any of the men as per your choice. Each question may only be answered by the man who has been asked the question out of the three men. Questions could be asked to the same man or different men. After getting the answers you must be able to identify which man is which. How can you do it? **(Level 3)**

100. You are one of the soldiers trapped behind enemy line. You would be rescued by a helicopter. On wireless set you come to know that helicopter will come exactly after 47 minutes. Then you lose contact. As soldiers are surrounded by enemy, helicopter has to fly low and cannot hover to search you. For the helicopter to locate your group you must fire two flair cartridges first red and then green when the helicopter is two minutes away from you, i.e. after 45 minutes. None of you have any working watch or device that can measure a time. Your life depends now on knowing exact 45 minutes from now. You have two slow-burning fuses, each of which will burn up in exactly one hour. They are not necessarily of the same length and width as each other, nor even necessarily of uniform width. So its length is not proportional to the time it burns. Others are confused

To derive full benefit, do not refer to the answer unless you make enough efforts to solve the puzzle.

LOGIRIDDLES

and give up any hope. But you quickly figure out what to do. Using these two fuses, how do you measure 45 minutes? **(Level 2)**

101. A man leaves home for his office at 1 pm on vehicle and reaches office at 3 pm. He had to stay at office throughout the day and night due to important and urgent work. The following day he departs from his office at 1 pm and gets home at 3 pm, by following the same path as the previous day in opposite direction. Obviously due to traffic he did not maintain same speed throughout his journey on both days. The speed was variable although he took same total time for both legs of his journey. Was he necessarily ever at the same point on the path at the same time on both days? **(Level 2)**

102. The town of Konigsberg (now Kaliningrad) was divided in four sections by branches of Pregel River. These four sections included two regions on the banks of Pregel, Kneiphof Island and the regions between the two branches of river. Seven bridges connected the regions. The figure below depicts the region and bridges. The people took a long walk through town on Sundays. They wondered whether it is possible to start at some location in the town, travel across all bridges without crossing any bridge twice, and return to the starting point. Is it possible? If yes how? If not, why not? **(Level 3)**

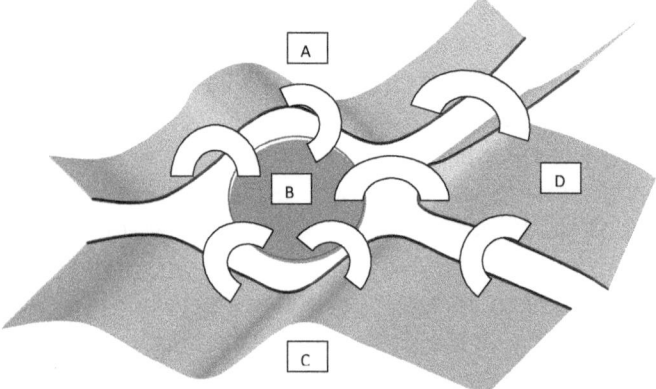

To derive full benefit, do not refer to the answer unless you make enough efforts to solve the puzzle.

103. Following figure has eight boxes. Fill these with eight numbers from 1 to 8, one in each box such that no two consecutive numbers are in the boxes touching each other. (Level 2)

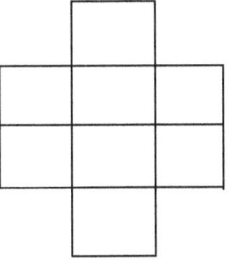

104. There are two suspects arrested for a crime. However, there is no substantial evidence to prove the major charge unless one of them confesses. The police keep the two suspects in separate cells and explain the consequences. If neither confesses, then both will be convicted of a minor offense and sentenced to one month in prison. If both confess, they will be sent to prison for six months. Finally, if only one of them confesses and turns approver, then he will be released while other will be sentenced to nine months in prison, six months for the crime and additional three months for obstructing the course of justice. What would you think the prisoners do?
(Level 2)

105. Take any map of districts, states, countries which is required to be coloured. Obviously we cannot use same colour for two adjacent districts, states or countries. Irrespective of the map, how many minimum numbers of colours are required to ensure correct painting of the map? (Level 1)

106. There are two trees A and B. Both have few birds. If one bird from the tree A flies to the tree B, number of birds on the tree B is double the number of birds on the tree A. Whereas, if one bird from the tree B flies to the tree A, number of birds on the tree B and the number of birds on the tree A become equal. How many birds are there on the trees A and B? (Level 1)

To derive full benefit, do not refer to the answer unless you make enough efforts to solve the puzzle.

LOGIRIDDLES

107. Can we draw the following picture (known as Mohammed's Scimitars) in a continuous motion without lifting a pencil so that no part of the picture is retraced? How? (Level 2)

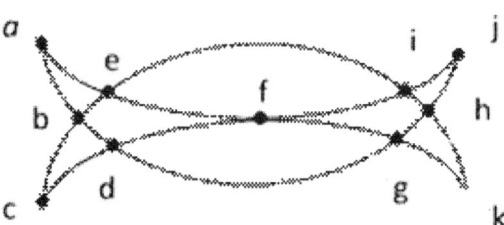

108. There are 3 pegs mounted on a board together with discs of different sizes. Initially these are placed on one peg in order of sizes with the largest on the bottom. The rule is to move discs one at a time from one peg to another as long as a disc is never placed on top of a smaller disc. The goal of the puzzle is to have all the discs on the other peg. Find minimum number moves required to transfer 8 discs from peg 1 to peg 2 without violating the rule. (Level 3)

109. You have one rectangular sheet of paper. This paper has one small rectangular portion cut and removed. The cut portion may be at any position on the paper and with any orientation. One such example is shown below. You are asked to cut the paper in two parts by a straight cut such that both the pieces of the paper would have same area. How will you make the cut? (Level 3)

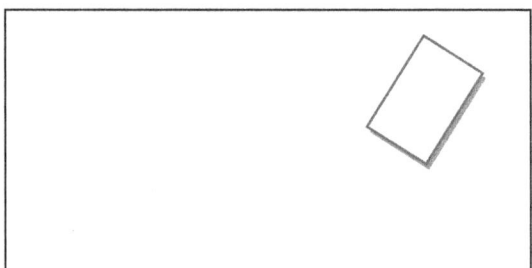

To derive full benefit, do not refer to the answer unless you make enough efforts to solve the puzzle.

110. There are two trees A and B. Both have few birds. If one bird from the tree A flies to the tree B, number of birds on the tree B is triple the number of birds on the tree A. Whereas, if one bird from the tree B flies to the tree A, number of birds on the tree B and the number of birds on the tree A become equal. How many birds are there on the trees A and B? (Level 1)

111. There are three locations A, B and C where three values X, Y and Z are stored respectively.

Location	A	B	C
Value Stored	X	Y	Z

We are allowed three operations as follows:

Operation	Meaning
C = A → C	Move value from A to C (or replace the value in C location by the value in A location)
C = B → C	Move value from B to C (or replace the value in C location by the value in B location)
A = A − C	Subtract the value at C location from the value at A location and then store the result in A location

If now using any of these operations in sequence you want value Y in the location A. How will you achieve it? (Level 2)

112. You have 'n' different numbers that are listed randomly. Consider n is large say more than 100. Now we want to find highest and lowest number amongst them. What is the minimum number of comparison operations required to find them on computer? Also describe the method. (Note that for finding highest or lowest number on computer we need to compare two numbers at a time. While running a program comparison operation is most time consuming. Hence number of comparison operations is called as time complexity of such sorting programs.) (Level 3)

To derive full benefit, do not refer to the answer unless you make enough efforts to solve the puzzle.

113. Given below is a shape of a fish swimming from left to right made out of matchsticks. Change the direction of the fish from right to left by moving only three matchsticks. Now change the direction of the fish by moving only two matchsticks. Do not worry about the heads of the matchsticks; they do not represent anything in this puzzle. **(Level 1)**

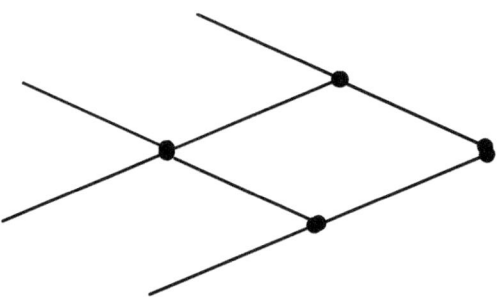

114. Given below is a shape of a wine glass made out of matchsticks. It has a smiley in it. Take out the smiley without touching it. You may move two matchsticks but still retain the shape of the wine glass made out of matchsticks. Do not worry about the heads of the matchsticks; they do not represent anything in this puzzle. **(Level 1)**

115. There is a narrow bridge whose width is adequate only for one horse to pass. Thus only one horse can cross the bridge at a time in any one direction. Four horse men each come to the center of the bridge from both sides and stop when there is a gap between them of

To derive full benefit, do not refer to the answer unless you make enough efforts to solve the puzzle.

only one horse. All four horses on each side were head to tail with no gap between them. Horses cannot move backwards. They can move forward. Also they can jump over one horse at a time. How will these horses cross the bridge? The situation is depicted with matchsticks below. Head of the matchstick depicts the head of the horse. **(Level 3)**

116. Deepak, Sandhya, Poorwa and Sourabh went to an ice-cream parlor. Each picked an ice-cream of a different flavour. The flavours were Mango, Keshar-Pista, Butter scotch and Chocolate. Deepak and Poorwa both do not like Keshar-Pista. The person who likes Chocolate is a girl. (Sandhya and Poorwa are girls.). Sandhya likes Butter scotch, but it is not her favorite flavour. Sandhya's favorite flavour is either Butter scotch or Mango, although she can have only one favorite flavour. Deepak likes Chocolate, but it is not his favorite flavour. **(Level 1)**

117. There are three boxes on a table. One of the boxes contains Gold and the other two are empty. A printed message contains on each box. One of the messages is true and the other two are lies.

    The first box says 'The Gold is not here'.
    The Second box says 'The Gold is not here'.
    The Third box says 'The Gold is in the Second box'.
    Which box has the Gold? **(Level 1)**

118. A school teacher had a strange method of teaching mathematics to his class of one hundred students. He has a board outside the room with one hundred switches. Each switch is connected with one bulb each inside the room. All the switches with their respective bulbs are numbered from 1 to 100. Initially all the bulbs are 'OFF' that teacher shows to the students. The teacher takes all the students outside the room. Then the teacher asks the first student to operate every switch once. Then he

LOGIRIDDLES

tells the second student to operate every second switch (alternate) remembering the table of 2 and operate it. The third student is to operate every third switch i.e. operates switches appearing in the table of 3. The fourth student follows the table of 4 operating switches with numbers figuring in that table and so on.

After the process is completed with the hundredth student, the teacher asks, "Which are the lights in the room 'ON' and How many?" **(Level 3)**

119. Find X in following table.

2	3	4	15	12
3	4	5	28	20
4	5	6	X	30
5	6	7	66	42
6	7	8	91	56

(Level 2)

120. I have Rs 50 with me. My account shows as follows:

	Money Spend Rs	Balance Rs
	20	30
	15	15
	9	6
	6	0
Total	50	51

Where from the one rupee came? **(Level 1)**

121. In a family of eight members, there are three married couples. Each couple has at least one child. All are sitting around a circular table. Find the family and sequence of sitting.

(i) A is the grandfather of F and sitting second to the left of his grandson.

(ii) B is the nephew of E and sitting second to the left of his father.

To derive full benefit, do not refer to the answer unless you make enough efforts to solve the puzzle.

(iii) D is the son of H and sitting third to the right of his sister.

(iv) G is the father of F and sitting second to the right of his brother-in-law.

(v) C is not sitting adjacent to her spouse. F is not opposite his/her mother.

(vi) No one in the family is a widow/widower.

(vii) No two males are sitting adjacent to each other.

(Level 2)

122. A lady buys goods worth Rs. 200 from a shop. (Shopkeeper selling the goods with zero profit). The lady gives him Rs.1000 note. The shopkeeper gets the change from next shop and keeps Rs. 200 for himself and returns Rs. 800 to the lady. Later the shopkeeper of the next shop comes with the Rs. 1000 note saying it is a counterfeit note and takes his money back. How much loss did the shopkeeper face? **(Level 1)**

123. In the plane, the points with integer coordinates are called lattice points. Suppose a flea in the plane jumps from one lattice point to another. Each jump is one unit to the right, one unit to the left, one unit up, or one unit down. If the flea starts at the origin and makes exactly 10 jumps, how many lattice points could possibly be the final landing place of the flea? **(Level 3)**

124. One day a tourist comes to the only hotel in a debt ridden town where the hotel owner, retailer, wholesaler and farmer were all in debt. The tourist kept a 1000 Rupee note on the table and went to inspect the rooms. Hotel owner took the note and rushed to pay his debt to the retailer. Retailer ran to pay the wholesaler. Wholesaler ran to pay the farmer. Farmer ran to pay off to the owner for the rooms he rented earlier. Hotel owner then kept the 1000 Rupee note back on the counter. The tourist by then came down, took his money and left as he did not like the rooms.

No one earned anything. But all are now out of debts!!!!! How did it happen? **(Level 2)**

125. The puzzle is told in 2014. Add your age to 49. Multiply the answer by 2. Add 5 to the answer. Multiply the answer by 50. Add 1764 to the answer. Subtract your birth year. Last two digits of the answer will be your age. Explain how? **(Level 1)**

126. We can buy 20 orange toffees for Rs 1, one coffee bite toffees for Rs 1 and one chocolate toffee for Rs 5. You have Rs 100 with you and want to buy 100 toffees to distribute to friends. How much of each could you buy if you have to spend your entire money, if you must buy each of the toffees? **(Level 1)**

127. How many squares are there in the following figure? **(Level 1)**

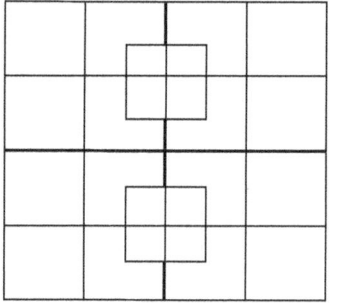

128. Poorwa and Nachiket just met Girish. They wanted to know when the Girish's birthday is. Girish gave them a list of 10 possible dates.

    May 15   May 16   May 19   June 17
    June 18   July 14   July 16   August 14
    August 15 August 17

    Girish then told Poorwa the month and Nachiket the date of his birthday. Poorwa and Nachiket then said:

    Poorwa: "I don't know when the Girish's birthday is, but I know that Nachiket does not know it too."

Nachiket: "At first I did not know when Girish's birthday is, but I know it now."

Poorwa: "A ha! Then now I also know when Girish's birthday is."

So can you tell when Girish's birthday is? **(Level 3)**

129. In a TV game show you have a group of three in a team. You are asked to stand one behind other such that the last person can see two of the team mates in front of him. The middle person can see the one in the front. The front person can see none of their team mates. They were shown five hats three white and two black. They are told that after they are blind folded three of the five caps would be put on their head, one hat for each member. Remaining two hats would be hidden. Then their blind folds would be removed. After that they can say whether they know the colour of the hat they are wearing or not. In case one of them can tell the colour of the hat he / she is wearing they win the game. They are not allowed to turn back or tell the other person the colour of his or her hat. As the game progresses and they are asked to tell the colour of their hats, the last person says "I don't know the colour of my hat". The middle person also says "I don't know the colour of my hat". At that stage the front person smiles and says "I know the colour of my hat". How is he / she so confident? What is the colour of his / her hat? **(Level 2)**

130. You have ten mangos in your basket. You meet ten friends. They ask mangos from you. You give one to each of your friends. Then suddenly you realize that there is one mango in the basket. How is it possible? **(Level 1)**

131. Five very intelligent friends get 100 gold coins in treasure hunt. They decide to divide the coins in a peculiar way. They decide that the senior most person by age would decide the distribution. Then they will vote. If the vote is at least 50% in the favour of the decision, the division is

final. However, if the vote is less that 50% in favour then the one who has given the division is disqualified and leaves empty handed. After that next senior most person by age continues the process. The process continues till the last when the last person keeps all the coins. All are genius and want to ensure they maximize their benefit. What would be the distribution? **(Level 3)**

132. Five very intelligent friends get 100 gold coins in treasure hunt. They decide to divide the coins in a peculiar way. They decide that the senior most person by age would decide the distribution. Then they will vote. However, the one who gives distribution is not allowed to vote. If the vote is at least 50% in the favour of the decision, the division is final. However, if the vote is less that 50% in favour then the one who has given the division is disqualified and leaves empty handed. After that next senior most person by age continues the process. The process continues till the last when the last person keeps all the coins. All are genius and want to ensure they maximize their benefit. What would be the distribution? **(Level 3)**

133. How many minimum linear cuts we have to take to cut a board of $m \times n$ squares in to 1×1 squares? **(Level 1)**

134. You have three bags. Each has two balls. One contains both Red balls, second contains one Red and one White ball, and the third contains both White balls. You don't know which has what balls. Without seeing you draw one ball from a randomly selected bag. This ball happens to be Red. Now what is the probability that the next ball from the same bag is Red. **(Level 2)**

135. Two towns Pune and Mumbai are exactly 160 km from each other. Prajakta and Deepak wanted to meet for some urgent work. To save time and one person's efforts they decide to travel from either side and meet on the road. Prajakta leaves Mumbai driving at average speed of 30 km/hr towards Pune. Deepak was held up for work

and leaves half an hour later than Prjakta. So to cover up delay he drives at average speed of 60 km/hr. Who is closer to Mumbai when they meet on the road?

(Level 1)

136. You have a birthday cake, round or rectangular for your birthday. You have your family members at the party. You are eight members including you. You need to cut the cake with a knife in three linear cuts so that you have eight pieces, one for each of you (may be with slight different sizes). **(Level 2)**

137. This is not a mathematical puzzle. So you don't have to be mathematician. It is a logic.

    Hint: You need to be observant.

    $9999 = 4$

    $8888 = 8$

    $1816 = 3$

    $1212 = 0$

    $1919 = ?$ **(Level 2)**

138. This puzzle is a logic with numbers.

    $5 - 4 = 23$

    $8 - 1 = 63$

    $6 - 16 = 32$

    $9 - 9 = 78$

    $3 - 9 = 6$

    $3 - 81 = ?$ **(Level 2)**

139. This is not a mathematical puzzle. So you don't have to be mathematician. It is a logic.

    $1111 = R$

    $2222 = T$

    $3333 = E$

    $4444 = N$

    $5555 = ?$ **(Level 3)**

To derive full benefit, do not refer to the answer unless you make enough efforts to solve the puzzle.

LOGIRIDDLES

140. This puzzle is deciphering a secret code.

　　January = 7110　　　February = 826
　　March = 5313　　　　April = 541
　　May = 3513　　　　　June = 4610
　　July = 4710　　　　　August = 681
　　September = ?　　　　　　　　　　　　(Level 2)

141. There were eight friends A, B, C, D, E, F, G and H in a room. A was ironing clothes. B was washing clothes. C was playing chess. D was taking bath. E was eating. F was studying. G was reading newspaper. What was H doing? (Level 1)

142. Use the numerals 1, 9, 9 and 6 exactly in that order to make the following numbers: 28, 32, 35, 38, 72, 73, 76, 77, 100 and 1000. You can also use mathematical operators +, -, ×, ÷, √, ^ (exponent) and brackets. All the numerals given above must be used once and only once. For example, 63 = 1×9+9×6 (level 2)

143. If　5 + 3+ 2 = 151022,
　　　9 + 2 + 4 = 183652,
　　　8 + 6 + 3 = 482466
　　　and 5 + 4 + 5 =202541
　　　Then 7 + 2 + 5 = ?.　　　　　　　　(Level 2)

144. A boy was sitting with his father and grandfather. Total of their age is 140 years. Number of months of age in respect of the boy is same as number of years of age of the grandfather. Number of days of age of the boy is same as number of weeks of age of the father. What are their ages in years? (Level 2)

145. Recycle firm observes that from three disposable milk cartons they can produce one milk carton by recycle process thus saving environment. From 81 new milk cartons after their use how many recycled milk cartons could be made and used? Can we say that from the production of new milk cartons 30% is recycled, thus

To derive full benefit, do not refer to the answer unless you make enough efforts to solve the puzzle.

saving environment by 30% damage due to disposable milk cartons? **(Level 1)**

146. There is a famous town where lot of star football players live, who had played in world cup tournaments in the past representing their country. We know that, a) No two players have scored same number of goals in world cup matches. b) No player has scored 15 goals in world cup matches. c) There are more star players who had represented country in world cup than the number of goals scored by any of these star player. So what is the maximum number of star players who represented their country in the world cup live in this town? **(Level 2)**

147. Fill the box using (1, 3, 5, 7, 9, 11, 13, 15). You can also repeat the numbers. You cannot use any arithmetic operator in the box. **(Level 2)**

    ☐ + ☐ + ☐ = 30

148. CEO of a big company came to factory early in the morning. He was greeted by a night watchman of the company who was just leaving for his home. The CEO told the watchman that he would be catching a flight shortly to Mumbai and would be back next day. The watchman requested the CEO not to take that flight but travel by road. When CEO asked reason, the watchman told him that in the night he had seen a scary dream in which that flight crashed while landing. He also informed the CEO that his dreams usually come true. CEO was superstitious and hence reluctantly took a car and drove to Mumbai. Next day morning he read the newspaper and to his shock there was the news of the crash of same flight where all the passengers were killed. He thanked the watchman. After returning back the General Manager also told CEO how his life was also saved earlier by the watchman in the same way. CEO immediately rewarded the watchman heftily and then sacked the watchman. Why did CEO do so? **(Level 1)**

To derive full benefit, do not refer to the answer unless you make enough efforts to solve the puzzle.

149. Two women and two doctors walked in an ice-cream parlor. All wanted Mango ice-cream. The parlor had only three Mango ice-creams left. However, all came out happily. How did it happen? **(Level 1)**

150. What is an object that maker doesn't need it, owner doesn't want it and user doesn't know he is using it. What is it? **(Level 2)**

151. Two fathers took their one son each to a fruit stall. All took one apple each and put them in a bag. When they reached home they found only three apples in the bag. They did not see anyone eating it or throwing it or dropping it. How was is it possible? **(Level 1)**

152. Tina, Meena and Leena were wives of Nandu, Chandu and Bandu (not in the corresponding order). They came to play badminton mixed doubles. But we do not know who the husband / wife of whom is? As per the rule of the tournament married couples were not allowed to be partners in the game. After the draw two pairs play the game and one sits outside. For the match Bandu's wife and Nandu became the partners. Tina's husband paired with Chandu's wife as a partner. Who was Tina's husband? **(Level 3)**

153. You are with a boat and can row at the speed of 10 km per hour in still water. With this boat you have to reach your friend who is 30 km upstream the river and collect a floating bobber. When you start, your friend with the idea to help you leaves the bobber in the stream so that it can flow down to you. The stream flows at the speed of 3 km per hour. After how many hours you get the bobber? **(Level 2)**

About this Part of the Book

I am sure that you have enjoyed solving this modest collection of 153 plus puzzles. As you have experienced, these puzzles are classified in three levels of difficulty. I expect most of the readers have solved the Level 1 puzzles are eager to check their answer. However, I suggest you to jot down the logic that you have used to solve them. May be your logic is more elegant that I have explained in this part. You may have found Level 2 puzzles are relatively difficult and many of you could solve them with some efforts. I am sure that you will get an insight to the logic of solving such puzzles once you read the answers. Don't get disheartened if you are unable to solve the Level 3 puzzles. You are among the majority. I would like to exhort you not to jump to see the answers unless you work on them for sufficient time. You could also take help of your friends or parents. Only when you are exhausted you may read the answers. Then make an effort to find a logical reason for the answer. Only after spending sufficient time, you read the logic behind the solution. This would give you satisfaction of exploring new things and also develop your logical thinking.

If you are parent, do not give part II to your children unless they make enough effort to solve them. First let children work on the puzzles, discuss them with friends. Then you give them answers one by one and ask them to find out how the answers are correct. Only then tell them the logic behind the answer. Discuss how the logic is correct. If you solve couple of puzzles per day, you would take few months to solve all. By then your logical skills would be sharpened.

Besides these direct advantages, with these puzzles in you armour, you could become very popular in any social gatherings as well as family function.

To derive full benefit, do not refer to the answer unless you make enough efforts to solve the puzzle.

I feel that this book would be interesting reading for people of all ages, senior school children, college students, working professionals, housewives, and retired people. For some it is learning, for others entertainment, for yet others amusement!! I am sure that it would be an enriching experience to the readers. So enjoy the solutions of the puzzles!!

Part 2

SOLUTIONS & LOGICAL EXPLANATIONS

To derive full benefit, do not refer to the answer unless you make enough efforts to solve the puzzle.

To derive full benefit, do not refer to the answer unless you make enough efforts to solve the puzzle.

LOGIRIDDLES

1. **Answer:** Take any six balls and put them in balance three on either side. There are two possibilities.

   a) Both sides are equal. In that case, remaining two balls have a defective ball. For second weighing take these two balls, one on either side. The one that is defective will be detected by balance going down on that side.

   b) If both sides are not equal, the one side that is heavy i.e. balance going down, has the defective ball among them. Take any two balls out that group and put one each side in balance. If balance goes down on either side, the side going down that ball is heavy (defective). If balance shows equal, the remaining third ball is heavy (defective).

   Note: For nine balls the procedure is same.

   Logic for Solution: In case of problems with balance there are always three possibilities. One side heavy, other side heavy or both sides equal. So every weighing we could split total group in three parts. Of course this is because we know that the defective ball is heavy. Also selecting balls for weighing, instead of half number of balls on either side, we could divide the total in three approximately equal groups. Then put two groups with equal number in either side of balance. This makes division faster and we can reach answer in least number of weighing. This process is common for number of puzzles.

2. **Answer:** ZERO.

   Logic for Solution: Don't get confused and jump and start using mathematics. The expression is a product of various terms. If you see carefully one term is (X-X) which is obviously zero. Hence the value of the expression is zero. In many aptitude questions you identifying these kinds of basics is the key.

3. **Answer:** Take any four balls out of eight. Put two on either side of the balance. There are two possibilities:-

To derive full benefit, do not refer to the answer unless you make enough efforts to solve the puzzle.

a) Both sides are equal: In that case the defective ball is in the remaining four balls not taken for weighing.
b) Both sides are un-equal: In that case defective ball is in these four.

Now put two balls from defective group on one side of the balance and two good balls on other side of the balance. There are two possibilities:-

a) Both sides are equal: In that case, the defective ball is among the remaining two balls from the defective group of four.
b) Both sides are not equal: In that case the two balls selected for weighing from the defective group have a defective ball.

Thus, in second weigh we have separated a group of two balls which has one defective. Now, the third weigh is simple. Take any one ball from defective group and put it in one side of the balance and one good ball on other side of the balance. There are two possibilities:-

a) Both sides are equal: In that case remaining ball from defective group of two is defective.
b) Both sides are not equal: In that case the ball selected for weighing from defective group is indeed defective.

Logic for Solution: In first weighing we can identify either the balls taken for weighing have the defective or the remaining balls have the defective. Both cases must be considered. Thus, we have reduced the problem by separating balls in two groups of four balls each. One group is known to have defective and other group is known to have good balls. Thus we bisected the group from eight to four to two to 1 separating the defective and good balls.

4. Answer:

   a) Cut the bar equal to one seventh and two seventh part of the gold bar with two cuts. Cuts are shown below.

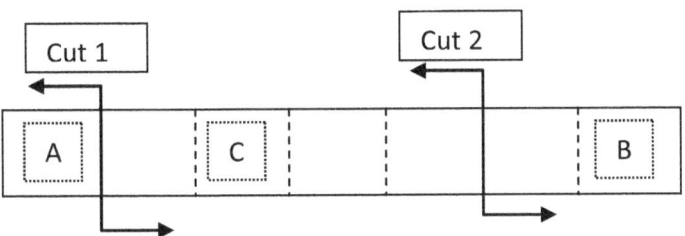

Thus there are three parts. Part A has one piece with weight 1/7 of the bar. Part B has two pieces of 1/7 weight of the bar. And third part C has four pieces of 1/7 weight of the bar. Now after first day give part A which is 1/7 weight of the bar. On second day give part B and take back part A so effectively giving additional 1/7 weight of the bar. On third day give part A. On fourth day give Part C and take back part A and part B. On fifth day give part A. On sixth day give part B and take back part A. On seventh day give part A. Thus we have paid equal amount every day and finally given complete gold bar by seventh day. We have cut the bar only twice.

   b) Another method that cuts the bar in seven equal weight pieces in two cuts. Of course this is bit complicated and may not be accepted in interviews. Nevertheless, it is creative!!!

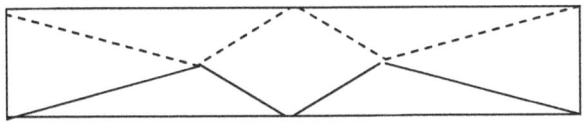

Logic for Solution: For these kinds of puzzles first identify how much is the smallest part we have to provide, call it one part. Then think of other parts like two parts. Start using combinations. Many problem of finding least coinage required to pay also fall in these kinds of puzzles. e.g. minimum number of coins and notes (tenders) required to pay up to certain amount.

To derive full benefit, do not refer to the answer unless you make enough efforts to solve the puzzle.

5. Answer:

Take any six balls from nine and call this as 'Group A'. Call the remaining three balls as 'Group B'. Out of the six balls from 'Group A' put three each on either side of balance. There are two possibilities:-

    a) Both sides are equal: In that case the defective is in remaining three balls from 'Group B'.

    b) Both sides are unequal: In that case the defective ball is in these six balls taken for under weighing. That is the defective ball is from the 'Group A'. We also note which side is down and which side is up. Call the side which is down as 'Group A1' and the side which is up as 'Group A2'. The defective ball could be heavy from 'Group A1' or light from 'Group A2'.

Now for second round of weighing take three balls each from both the groups i.e. 'Group B' and 'Group A1' and put them for weighing on either side of the balance. We have already identified the group which has all non-defective balls. So in second weighing we know which side of the balance is standard. There are two possibilities depending on the result of the first weighing.

    a) The group that has three balls (Group B) is defective. In this case we know that in second weighing one of the sides with these three balls of 'Group B' would go down or up, since the other side has three balls from non-defective group. In this weighing we will know whether the defective ball in 'Group B' is heavy or light.

    b) The group that has six balls (Group A) is defective. In this case there are two possibilities:-

    i) Both sides are equal. In this case we can conclude that 'Group A2' has the defective ball. We also know that the defective ball must be light.

    ii) Both sides un-equal: Since one side has all the three good balls from 'Group B', we can conclude that the defective ball is in 'Group A1' and the defective ball is heavy.

To derive full benefit, do not refer to the answer unless you make enough efforts to solve the puzzle.

The third weighing is simple. We have already identified the group of three balls which has one defective ball. We also know from the second weighing whether the defective ball is heavy or light. Now take two balls from the defective group and put them one on each side of balance. There are two possibilities:-

a) Both sides are equal: In that case the third ball that was left out is defective. Whether defective ball is heavy or light is already known in the second weighing.

b) Both sides are unequal: Since we already know whether the defective ball is heavy or light. If it was known that the defective ball is light then the side of the balance that goes up has the defective ball. If it was known that the defective ball is heavy then the side of the balance that goes down has the defective ball.

Thus in three weighing we have identified the defective ball and also it is heavy or light.

Logic for Solution: In the first weighing nine balls are split in three group of three each. After first weighing we either segregated three defective balls or three non-defective balls with additional information that among the defective group which subgroup is heavy and which one is light.

In second weighing we have extracted additional information to ascertain whether the defective ball is heavy or light and also segregated the defective subgroup of three balls. Thus we have identified the group of three balls which is defective and also whether the defective ball is heavy or light. Now it is very simple like the first puzzle to find out the defective ball.

6. **Answer:**   1. India   2. Pakistan   3. Sri Lanka

Logic for Solution: Let us consider Kunal's report. If his statement about Pakistan coming second is false, His statement that Sri Lanka won the tournament is correct. In that case Sourabh's both statements prove to be false. Hence this cannot be the correct answer.

_{To derive full benefit, do not refer to the answer unless you make enough efforts to solve the puzzle.}

On the other hand if Kunal's statement about Sri Lanka winning the tournament is false, His statement that Pakistan coming second is correct. Now Sourabh's second statement of Sri Lanka coming second has to be false. Therefore, his first statement must be correct. This does not contradict Kunal's case of one false and one correct statement. Hence we get the result as indicated.

7. **Answer:** A & B crosses with flashlight: Time 2 minutes. Then B Returns alone with flashlight: Time 2 minutes. Then C & D crosses with flashlight: Time 10 minutes. Then A Returns alone with flashlight: Time 1 minute. Then A & B crosses with flashlight: Time 2 minutes. Now all have crossed. Total time is $2 + 2 + 10 + 1 + 2 = 17$ minutes.

(Now watch the bridge collapse? You will never see something like this in your life!!!)

Logic for Solution: Since flashlight is one and only two people can cross together, we need two return trips to carry the flashlight back. Hence we will need three forward trips of pairs for original four people plus two people who would have returned with flashlight.

If C and D go in a separate trip, total time spent is $10 + 5 = 15$ minutes for two trips, 10 minutes for the pair containing C and 5 minutes for the pair containing D. Minimum two return trips would require $1 + 1 = 2$ minutes. Also the last trip of a pair would take at least 2 minutes. This would make total time of 19 minutes. Thus if we want to complete the crossing in 17 minutes C and D must cross together. This is the crux of the solution.

After they cross, obviously one of them cannot make return trip as it would result in total time more than 20 minutes. Hence, before C & D cross together, either A or B must have crossed so as to make the return trip. Therefore the first crossing must be done by A & B.

Then one of them returns with flashlight. Then C & D cross. Then the remaining person from A & B returns with flashlight.

Finally, A & B cross together. Thus the total time is 10 minutes for C & D crossing, 2 + 2 = 4 minutes for twice crossing of A & B and 1 + 2 = 3 minutes for return trips of A & B individually. This totals to 17 minutes.

8. **Answer:** Total 7: Siblings consisting one boy, two girls; their parents, and parents of the father.

Logic for Solution: In such puzzles identify the inter relations.

9. **Answer:** 96

Logic for Solution: For winner to be decided 96 teams must lose. In every match one team loses. So to decide the winner 96 games must be played.

10. **Answer:** 3 draws.

Logic for Solution: This is a problem of pigeon-hole principle. There are two pigeon holes; one for black socks and one for white socks. There must be 3 pigeons to guarantee two pigeons in one of the hole. Hence the answer is three. Alternatively, consider we draw first and second socks. It could be a pair or in worst case it could be one white and one black. Hence we cannot guarantee a pair. Now when we draw third socks, it has to be either white or black. In any case it has to make a pair with one of the two we have drawn if they were not of the same colour already. In either case we will have a pair. So we can guarantee a pair in three draws.

11. **Answer:** Neha's birthday must be on 31stDecember of some year.

Logic for the Solution: Let's say she was born on 31stDecember 1990. That means Neha's ninth birthday is 31stDecember 1999. Let todayis1stJanuary 2000. Therefore two days earlier; that is on30thDecember 1999, Neha was indeed 8 years old. The 'Next year' is 2001 because this year is 2000. On 31stDecember 2001 which is next year, she will be 11 years old.

To derive full benefit, do not refer to the answer unless you make enough efforts to solve the puzzle.

12. Answer: Four half-full barrels are dumped into two of the empty barrels. This results in nine full barrels, three half-full barrels, and nine empty barrels. Each son gets three full barrels, one half-full barrel, and three empty barrels.

Logic for Solution: Total barrels are 21 and total wine is 7 full and 7 half i.e. total of 10 and a half. For dividing equally to three sons we need to distribute 3 and a half barrels of wine to each son. Also we need to give total of 7 barrels to each son. Therefore each son must get three full barrels one half filled barrel and remaining three empty barrels. Means we must have 9 full barrels, three half-filled barrels and 9 empty barrels. Originally we have 7 full, 7 half and 7 empty barrels. So we can get additional two full barrels and reduce four half-filled barrels by empting four half-filled barrels in two empty barrels. Now we have required number of barrels for equal distribution.

13. Answer: German keeps fish. He lives in green house, smokes Prince and drinks coffee.

Logic for Solution: First arrange the houses in terms of colours. (It is easy to work on colours from the statements). Hint 9 states 'The Norwegian lives in the first house'. Also hint 14 states 'The Norwegian lives next to the blue house'. This implies that the Second house is of Blue colour. Also hint 4 states 'The green house is on the left of the white house (it also means they are next door to each other)'. The hint 5 says 'The green house owner drinks coffee' and hint 8 states 'The man living in the house right in the center drinks milk' therefore the green house cannot be in the center. It can neither be the first as white house must be next to it and second house is known to be Blue. Hence the Green colour house is Fourth and White house is Fifth. Hint 1 says The 'British lives in a red house'. The first house is of Norwegian. Therefore, the Red house of the British must be the Third (Center). The only colour not yet identified is Yellow and it must of the first house. Thus the houses in order from left to right have colours as Yellow, Blue, Red, Green and White. The order in which the information is filled so far is shown by alphabets.

LOGIRIDDLES

Now we draw a Table and fill the information from the hints. We fill the fact of colours and other facts in systematic way in order given below.

Colour	Yellow (G)	Blue (B)	Red (F)	Green (C)	White (D)
Nationality	Norwegian (A)	Dane (Q)	British (E)	German (R)	Swede (U)
Beverage	Water (L)	Tea (P)	Milk (J)	Coffee (H)	Beer (N)
brand of cigar	Dunhill (I)	Blend (M)	Pall Mall (T)	Prince (S)	Blue Master (O)
Pet	Cats (X)	Horses (K)	Birds (W)	FISH	Dogs (V)

1: The British lives in a red house. **Fill British.** (Already filled)

5: The green house owner drinks coffee. **Fill Coffee.** (H)

7: The owner of the yellow house smokes Dunhill. **Fill Dunhill. (I)**

8: The man living in the house right in the center drinks milk. **Fill Milk. (J)**

9: The Norwegian lives in the first house. **Fill Norwegian.** (Already filled)

11: The man who keeps horses lives next to the man who smokes Dunhill. **Fill Horses. (K)**

3: The Dane drinks tea and

12: The owner who smokes Blue Master drinks beer. This clearly indicates that Norwegian does not drink tea or beer. Hence, obviously, Norwegian drinks water. **Fill Water. (L)**

15: The man who smokes Blend has a neighbor who drinks water. Hence, person in Blue house smokes Blend. **Fill Blend. (M)**

12: The owner who smokes Blue Master drinks beer. Hence it cannot be owner of Blue house who could

To derive full benefit, do not refer to the answer unless you make enough efforts to solve the puzzle.

drink Beer. Therefore, the owner of the White house who drinks Beer. Fill Beer and Fill Blue Master in white house. Also the remaining beverage i.e. Tea should be in Blue house. **Fill Tea. (N) & (P)**

3: The Dane drinks tea. **Fill Dane** in Blue house. (Q)

13: The German smokes Prince. So only place German and 'Prince' brand cigar can fit is in Green house. **Fill German** and **Prince**. indicated as (R) & (S). Now we can fill remaining brand of cigar 'Pall Mall' in Red house. **Fill Pall Mall**. indicated as (T). Similarly the last vacant cell for nationality can be filled by Swede. **Fill Swede. (W)**

2: The Swede keeps dogs as pets. **Fill Dogs** as pet. (V)

6: The person who smokes Pall Mall rears birds. **Fill Birds. (W)**

10: The man who smokes Blend lives next to the one who keeps cats. Hence the Cats must be the pets in Norwegian's house. **Fill Cats. (X)**

Only cell left for Fish is in Green house owned by a German.

14. Answer: Fifty eight minutes.

Logic for Solution: Net progress of the goat is one foot per minute; (3 – 2 =1). Therefore the goat reaches at the height of fifty seven feet in fifty seven minutes. Next in one minutes the goat climbs three feet and reaches the top. Now since goat has already reached top he would not slip back (or since goat has already reached top slipping back two feet is not consequential to the puzzle).

15. Answer: Keep one White in one bowl and rest all in other bowl.

Probability = $(1/2)*(1) + (1/2)*(49/99) = 0.7474$

Logic for Solution: Now probability of choosing any bowl is half. So the probability of choosing white marble is the sum of the probability of choosing the bowl i.e. half in each case multiplied by probability of choosing white marble in that bowl.

Highest probability of choosing a white marble is 1 if that bowl does not have a black marble. For this just one white marble in one of the bowl is enough. Increasing white marbles in that bowl does not increase probability of choosing white marble in that bowl but on the other hand reduces the probability of choosing white marble in other bowl. Hence it is not efficient. Adding black marble in the bowl that has only white marble reduces the probability of picking white marble drastically without increasing the same significantly in other bowl.

16. Answer: 10 steps.

Logic for Solution: With high as well as low tide, ship goes up or down with water as it is floating. Ladder is attached to the ship. So it will remain at same position relative to the water.

17. **Answer: A is taller than B if we do not consider that people can have same height.**

    If people can have same height, A is taller or equal to the height of B. (In other words A cannot be shorter than B)

Logic for Solution: Let a_{ij} indicate the height of a person in i^{th} row and j^{th} column. Now we select tallest person among each row. Suppose the shortest among them is from k^{th} row. We call him A. Let his height be X. Now since A is among the tallest in k^{th} row, all others in that row would be shorter than him.

Now we select the shortest among each column. Suppose the tallest among them is in m^{th} column. We call him B. Let his height be Y. Now the B is at position a_{km} i.e. in K^{th} row or at any position other than in K^{th} row. If it is in K^{th} row, we know that $X > a_{km}$, because the element A is the tallest in k^{th} row. Hence $X > Y$. In other words A is taller than B.

Suppose the element B is in any other row than K but in m^{th} column, $Y < a_{km}$, because B is the shortest element in m^{th} column. But we know that $X > a_{km}$. Hence, in this case '$X > a_{km} > Y$'. This implies $X > Y$. In other words A is taller than B.

<small>To derive full benefit, do not refer to the answer unless you make enough efforts to solve the puzzle.</small>

Note 1: If people can have same height, there is a possibility that out of two people who are tallest in their respective rows and have a tie for shortest among tallest. Once we select one of them as A, the other may be the shortest in its column. Then obviously he would be tallest among shortest i.e. B. In this case A and B would be of same height.

Note 2: If A is same is B, it is called as a saddle point.

18. Answer: a) First fill milk in 5 liter measure. b) Then pour from it in 3 liter measure. c) Then empty the 3 liter measure back in the tank. d) Pour the remaining 2 liter milk from 5 liter measure in 3 liter measure. Now 3 liter measure has 2 liters milk and 5 liter measure is empty. e) Fill 5 liter measure from the tank. f) Pour 1 liter milk from 5 liter measure in to 3 liter measure till it gets filled. Thus we have poured 1 liter milk in remaining space of 3 liter measure. Now we have 4 liter milk left in the 5 liter measure. This we can give it to the customer. The total steps are 6. These are minimum number of steps.

We also have another method. a) First fill the milk in 3 liter measure. b) Empty this 3 liters milk in 5 liter measure. c) Again fill the 3 liters measure. d) Pour 2 liters of milk from 3 liter measure in empty space of 5 liter measure till it gets filled. Now 3 liter measure has 1 liter milk. e) Empty 5 liter measure in the tank. f) Pour remaining 1 liter milk from 3 liter measure in the 5 liter measure. g) Fill the 3 liter measure from the tank. f) Pour this 3 liters milk in the 5 liter measure which already had 1 liter milk. Thus now 5 liter measure has 4 liters milk. This we can give it to the customer. This method has taken 7 steps. Hence the first process is quicker.

Note: In another variation if we cannot put the milk in the tank and has to throw the milk while emptying the measure, in first method we have to throw only 3 liters where as in second method we have to throw 5 liters. Thus from this aspect also the first method is superior.

To derive full benefit, do not refer to the answer unless you make enough efforts to solve the puzzle.

Note: There is another intelligent solution. This was found out by my one of the student. This is applicable only if the measure is symmetric in shape. In this case tilt the 5 liter measure diagonally while filling. Now we can fill the measure exactly half as shown below.

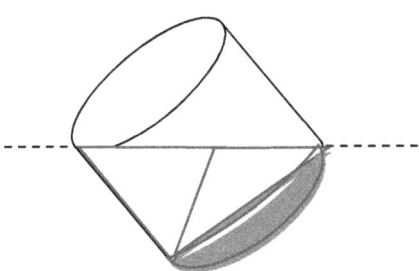

Now 5 liter measure has two and a half liter milk. Similarly in 3 liter measure we can fill one and half liter milk. If we pour one and half liter milk in two and half liter in five liter measure, we have four liter milk. This is what we wanted.

Logic for Solution: We have measures of 3 liters and 5 liters volume. We need to make 4 liters by combinations of these volumes by addition and subtraction. We can make it as,

$4 = 3 - (5 - 3) + 3$

19. Answer: In the morning everyone sees all other persons and count mathematicians with mark on forehead. Suppose a particular mathematician counts the total as X. Then he would keep counting the shuttle of horse coaches. If no one goes in Xth shuttle then when $(X + 1)$th shuttle comes he gets in it and goes for the party. For example if he counts 10 marks, and no one boards 10th shuttle, he boards in 11th shuttle and goes for the party.

Logic for Solution: Firstly the mathematicians realize that minimum one person is invited and maximum all are invited. Also they know that everyone is equally intelligent and hence believe that no one would make a wrong move. Now suppose only one is invited, then only one mathematician, say 'A', has a mark on his forehead. So 'A' will see nobody with mark and all others will see one person i.e. 'A' with mark. Since 'A' sees no one with mark, he realizes that he is the only one invited. So he boards the first shuttle. (Note than for 'A' X = 0, hence X + 1 = 1). Since 'A' boards the shuttle, no one else will board any shuttle thereafter. (Note that for all others X = 1, hence X + 1 = 2. But they would have boarded second shuttle only if nobody had boarded first shuttle. In this case 'A' has boarded the first shuttle, so others boarding second or further shuttle do not arise). Suppose there are two mathematicians are invited, say 'A' and 'B'. Now only 'A' and 'B' would count one mathematician with mark. All others would count two. Nobody would board the first shuttle as nobody has counted zero marks on forehead. So both 'A' and 'B' would board second shuttle. (For them X = 1, hence X+1 = 2). Since 'A' and 'B' board the second shuttle, there is no question of others boarding third shuttle although they have counted two marks. You can extend this logic for any number of invitees up to 20 i.e. all mathematicians.

Note: This logic is not applicable if no one is invited.

20. Answer: 760

Logic for Solution:

There are 40 people in the party. We can form,

$\binom{40}{2} = \frac{40!}{2! \times 38!} = \frac{40 \times 39}{2} = 20 \times 39$ Un-ordered pairs.

Of these 20 are couples (husband and wife) that must be subtracted to satisfy the given condition of handshakes. Thus the number of possible handshakes under condition is,

$$20 \times 39 - 20 = 20 \times 38 = 760$$

21. **Answer:** a) First fill milk in 5 liter measure. b) Then pour the milk from it in 3 liter measure. c) Pour the remaining 2 liters milk from the 5 liter measure in to customer's container. d) Then empty the 3 liter measure back in to 5 liter measure. e) Fill the remaining 2 liter milk from tank to 5 liter measure. f) Then pour the milk from it in 3 liter measure. g) Pour the remaining 2 liters milk from the 5 liter

measure in to customer's container. Now the customer has 4 liter milk as required. The total steps are 7. These are minimum number of steps. (Of course we have now 3 liters milk with us that cannot be poured back! Let us drink it!!)

Logic for Solution: We have measures of 3 liters and 5 liters volume. We need to make 4 liters by combinations of these volumes by addition and subtraction. We can make it as,

$4 = (5 - 3) + (5 - 3)$

22. Answer: 49

Logic for Solution: Now to form a rectangle from four squares, we need one center point that touches all squares. In 8 X 8 chess board we have 7 X 7 = 49 such internal points. Thus we can select four squares to form rectangles in 49 ways.

23. Answer:

a) Chances of survival are 50:50 (i.e. half). Expected number of days to come out is seven.

b) Chances have improved. Expected number of days to come out is five.

c) Now survival is certain. Expected number of days to come out is three.

Logic for Solution:

a) Let the number of days to come out of the cave be X. Let average number of days (expected value) to come out is $E(X)$. Note that $E(X) = \Sigma_i X_i P_i$, where X_i is number of days to go out from the path and Pi is probability of selecting that path. Now since all paths are identical the probability is equal as 1/3 for all the paths. Also note that from two of the paths he reaches the original place and then again the expected value is $E(X)$ as earlier. So we write the equation as,

$E(X) = \Sigma X_i P_i = \frac{1}{3} \times [E(X) + 3] + \frac{1}{3} \times [E(X) + 3] + \frac{1}{3} \times 1 = \frac{2}{3} \times E(X) + \frac{7}{3}$

Or, $E(X) = 7$

To derive full benefit, do not refer to the answer unless you make enough efforts to solve the puzzle.

Thus the average number of days to come out is seven. Since the food, water and flash light is only enough for seven days the chances of survival are 50:50 (i.e. half).

b) Let E(X) be the original expected value to come out. Let E(X1) is the expected value to come out after first try from the wrong path.

$$E(X) = \sum X_i P_i = \frac{1}{3} \times [E(X_1) + 3] + \frac{1}{3} \times [E(X_1) + 3] + \frac{1}{3} \times 1 = \frac{2}{3} \times E(X_1) + \frac{7}{3}$$

Or, $E(X) = \frac{2}{3} \times E(X_1) + \frac{7}{3}$

However, after first failed attempt, adventurer would not use the path by which he has just come back. Hence he has only two paths as options.

$$E(X_1) = \frac{1}{2} \times [E(X_1) + 3] + \frac{1}{2} \times 1 = \frac{1}{2} \times E(X_1) + 2$$

Or, $E(X_1) = 4$

Substituting,

$$E(X) = \frac{2}{3} \times 4 + \frac{7}{3} = 5$$

c) Now the adventurer could mark his first entry with marker. If he comes back to the original place he knows which path to avoid. He would obviously avoid the path he had just returned as well as the marked path. So he can go out from the correct path and come out in one more day. So, he would take maximum four days and minimum one day. So he will certainly survive. To calculate average number of days to come out,

$$E(X) = \sum X_i P_i = \frac{1}{3} \times [3 + 1] + \frac{1}{3} \times [3 + 1] + \frac{1}{3} \times 1 = 3$$

24. **Answer:** First, label the containers of all the batches from 1 to 50. Now take one ball from the first batch, two balls from the second batch, three balls from the third batch, and so on till 50 balls from the fiftieth batch. Now weigh all the selected balls. From the total weight of selected balls in grams, subtract 12750 (or from 12750 subtract total weight if defective balls have less weight). Divide the answer by 0.2. The resulting number is the batch number which has defective balls.

To derive full benefit, do not refer to the answer unless you make enough efforts to solve the puzzle.

Logic for Solution: If all the batches were without defect with all balls weighing 10 gm each, the total weight would have been, 10×1275=12750 gms. However one of the batches has defective balls with weight of each ball is either heavier or lighter by 0.2 gm. Thus the total weight is more (or less) by the amount depending upon the number of balls selected from that batch multiplied by 0.2. To differentiate between batches we have selected different number of balls from each batch. Since the error in each defective ball is known to be 0.2 gm the total error is 0.2 multiplied by the defective balls selected for weighing.

Note: The answer part in bracket is for a separate puzzle with defective balls having less weight.

25. **Answer:** 1201556593× 10^{16}

Logic for Solution: Now first card can be drawn in 52 ways. If repetition is to be avoided, we draw the next card without replacing the earlier drawn card. Thus, second card can be drawn in 51 ways. We proceed in this way till we draw 9 cards. Then for the 10th card to repeat it must come from any of the first nine cards already drawn. This can be done in 9 ways. Hence number of ways of drawing 10 cards with 10th card as the first to be repeated is,

$$52 \times 51 \times 50 \times \ldots \times 45 \times 44 \times 9 = 1201556593 \times 10^{16}$$

26. **Answer:** We will prove it using mathematical induction. Let us consider a palindrome of even length 2k, where k is an integer. Let us assume that the result is true for (k – 1), i.e. the palindrome of even length 2(k – 1) or (2k – 2) is divisible by 11. Now the number can be expressed as sum of digits multiplied by the place value as,

$$N = a_{2k-1} \times 10^{2k-1} + a_{2k-2} \times 10^{2k-2} + a_{2k-3} \times 10^{2k-3} + \cdots + a_0 \times 10^0$$
$$N = (a_{2k-1} \times 10^{2k-1} + a_0 \times 10^0) + (a_{2k-2} \times 10^{2k-2} + a_{2k-3} \times 10^{2k-3} + \cdots + a_1 \times 10^1)$$
$$N = (a_{2k-1} \times 10^{2k-1} + a_0 \times 10^0) + 10 \times (a_{2k-2} \times 10^{2k-3} + a_{2k-3} \times 10^{2k-4} + \cdots + a_1 \times 10^0)$$

Since the number is a palindrome, $a_{2k-1}=a_0, a_{2k-2}=a_1, a_{2k-3}=a_2$, and so on. Therefore,

$$N = a_{2k-1} \times (10^{2k-1} + 1) + 10 \times (a_{2k-2} \times 10^{2k-3} + a_{2k-3} \times 10^{2k-4} + \cdots + a_{2k-2} \times 10^0$$
$$= a_{2k-1} \times P + Q$$

Where P is a number of '2k' length that has first and last digit as 1 and remaining digits as 0, and Q is a palindrome of length (2k − 2) = 2(k − 1).

Now since we have assumed that the result is true for (k − 1), i.e. the palindrome of even length 2(k − 1) or (2k -2) is divisible by 11, implies that Q is divisible by 11. Hence,

$$N = a_{2k-1} \times (10000\ldots0001) + 11 \times R$$

Where R is an integer.

Now, $(10000\ldots0001) = 11 \times (909090\ldots9091)$

Where, $(10000\ldots0001)$ is of length 2k and $(909090\ldots9091)$ is of length of (2k − 2). Thus,

$N = a_{2k-1} \times 11 \times (9090\ldots9091) + 11 \times R = 11 \times$
$[a_{2k-1} \times (9090\ldots9091) + R]$

As we can see that N is divisible by 11. Hence the result is true for the palindrome of length k. Thus if the result is true for (k − 1) we have proved that it is true for k. Now, for k = 1 the result is obvious but trivial as the palindrome is of length 0. For k = 2, (2k − 2) = 2. Now, palindromes of length 2 are, 11, 22, 33, 44, 55, 66, 77, 88 and 99. We can see that all are divisible by 11. Thus we have proved that the result is true for k = 2. Hence it is true for 3, 4, ... for any integer. Thus we have proved that N is divisible by 11.

27. **Answer:**   i) 204   ii) 1296

Logic for Solution:

i) Small squares (of one size) could be chosen in 8 ways along length and 8 ways along width, thus in 82 ways. For squares of width two we have 7 ways to choose along length and 7 ways along width, giving total of 72 ways. Proceeding in this way till finally, there is 1 square of size eight (full chess board). Then using product and sum rule, total number of squares of various sizes is,

$$8^2 + 7^2 + 6^2 + \cdots + 2^2 + 1^2 = \frac{8 \times 9 \times 17}{6} = 204$$

ii) In case of rectangle of any size, first we consider rectangles of width one along with length one in 8 ways or length 2 in 7 ways, ……..length 8 in one way. Width one can be selected in 8 ways. Thus, the total number of rectangles of width one is, 8×(8+7+…+2+1)

Similarly we can consider rectangles of width two along with length one in 8 ways, length 2 in 7 ways, etc. Width two can be selected in 7 ways. Proceeding in this way and using product and sum rules appropriately. Number of rectangle (including squares) is,

8×(8+7+…+2+1)+7×(8+7+…+2+1)+…+1×(8+7+…+2+1)
=(8+7+…+2+1)×(8+7+…+2+1)= 36^2=1296

Note: If we want to exclude squares from the rectangle answer would be 1296 – 204 = 1092

28. Answer: 448

Logic for Solution: By symmetry number of ways to place two identical rooks in a common row is same as that of column. Number of ways of placing two rooks on two of the 8 squares in any column is 8C2 =28. There are 8 columns. Therefore, number of ways to place two identical rooks in a common column is 8 X 28 = 224. Similarly adding result for the rows, we get, required result as, 224 + 224 = 448

29. Answer: 1288

Logic for Solution: Here we first find the number of ways where two small squares are on same column or row or diagonal. Then by subtracting it from total selection of two squares, we can get the answer. Since two queens are identical we first solve the problem for ordered pair and then divide by 2! = 2.

First we select a place for one queen. This can be done in 64 ways. Then number of ways of selecting another square in a column is 7. Hence number of ways of selecting two squares in a column is, 64 X 7 = 448. By Symmetry we get same answer for rows. Thus, total number of selecting two squares in same row is 448.

In case of diagonals if we select one place on first or last row/column, number of places on diagonals is 7. There are 28 squares on first or last row/column. Thus, by product rule, number of ways to select two squares on common diagonal = 28X7 = 196.

Similarly for squares on 2nd and 7th row/column, number of squares on diagonals is 9 and number of places on 2nd and 7th row/column is 20. Thus number of ways to select two squares on common diagonal is 20 X 9 = 180.

Continuing in this way for 3rd and 6th row/column it is, 12 X 11 = 132 and for 4th and 5th row/column it is 4 X13 = 52.

Thus total ways of selecting 2 squares in common row or column or diagonal is,

= 448+448+196+180+132+52= 1456

One place on the board can be selected in 64 ways. After selecting the first square, second can be selected out of any of the remaining 63 squares. Thus by product rule, total number of selecting any two squares on the chess board is 64X63 = 4032

Hence total ways of selecting 2 squares in common row or column or diagonal is,

4032 – 1456 = 2576 ways.

This answer is true if the two queens are different (say white and black). Since in the puzzle two queens are identical we need to divide the answer by 2! = 2

Hence number of places 2 identical queens on a 8 X 8 chess board can be placed so that they are not placed in common row or column or diagonal is,

2576/2 = 1288

_{To derive full benefit, do not refer to the answer unless you make enough efforts to solve the puzzle.}

30. Answer: 1568

Logic for Solution: The logic is same as above except that we do not subtract number of ways the squares are on same diagonal. Thus, number of ways can two small size squares be selected from 8 X 8 chess board so that they are not in the same row or same column is, (4032 – 448 – 448)/2 = 1568

31. Answer: 634256

Logic for Solution: In this case we subtract number of ways to select four small size squares all in the same column or row from total number of ways to select four small size squares on 8 X 8 chess board. This is, $_{46}C_4 - 2X8X\ _8C_4 = 634256$

32. Answer: a) 112 b) 232

Logic for Solution:

a) For two adjacent squares we have a common line. For small squares we have 8 X 7 = 56 vertical and 56 horizontal common lines. Hence the answer is 112

b) If we consider the squares of different sizes and count common vertical lines separating adjacent squares, we get number of such lines corresponding to the sizes of one by one, two by two, three by three and four by four as, 8 X 7 + 7 X 5 + 6 X 3 + 5 X 1 = 56 + 35 + 18 + 5 = 116

By symmetry number of squares separated by horizontal lines is also 116.

Thus, different ways two adjacent squares of any sizes that can be selected from 8 X 8 chessboard is, 232

33. Answer: 7

Logic for Solution:
We know that, $441000 = 2^3 \times 3^2 \times 5^3 \times 7^2$

Now consider a set $X = \{2^3, 3^2, 5^3, 7^2\}$ If we partition these four elements in two unordered parts and multiply them, we will

To derive full benefit, do not refer to the answer unless you make enough efforts to solve the puzzle.

get two relatively prime factors of 441000. Such partition can be (1/3)or (2/4). Now using formula for ordered partition of 4 elements in these parts, number of ways of doing this is,

$$\frac{4!}{3!1!} + \frac{4!}{2!2!} = 7$$

34. Answer: a) 485 b) 514

Logic for Solution: To find leap years we need to find years divisible by 4 of these years divisible by 100 to be reduced in that years divisible by 400 to be added,

a) $(750-30+7) - (250-10+2) = 485$
b) $(1001 - 40 + 10) - (471 - 18 + 4) = 514$

35. Answer: The man has dined 16 times in restaurant.

Logic for Solution: Let N= number of times the man had dined. By inclusion-exclusion

Thus, $8 = N - 12 + 6 - 4 + 3 - 2 + 1$
Or, $N = 16$

36. Answer: 102

Logic for Solution: There are 101 grades possible. By the Pigeonhole principle among any 102 students there must be at least 2 students with the same score.

37. Answer: Let a_j is the number of games played on or before j^{th} day of the month. Then $a_1, a_2, \ldots, a_{30}$ is an increasing sequence of distinct positive integers, with $1 \leq a_j \leq 45$ More over, a sequence obtained by adding 14 to each of the numbers in this sequence namely $a_1+14, a_2+14, \ldots, a_{30}+14$, is also an increasing sequence of distinct positive integers, with $1 \leq a_j+14 \leq 49$

Now, these 60 positive integers $a_1, a_2, \ldots, a_{30}, a_1+14, a_2+14, \ldots, a_{30}+14$ are all less than or equal to 59. Hence by pigeonhole principle two of these integers are equal. Since a_j j=1, 2,......30 are all distinct such that $a_i = a_j +14$. That is $a_i - a_j = 14$. This means that exactly 14 games were played from day $(j+1)^{th}$ day to i^{th} day. Or there must be a period of some number of consecutive days; $(j+1)^{th}$ day to i^{th} day; during which the team must play exactly 14 games.

38. **Answer:** Let A be one of the six people of the five other people in the group. From the generalized pigeonhole with five people other than A and two possibilities viz. 'Friend of A' and 'Enemy of A', at least one possibility has 3 people. Therefore, there are either three or more who are friends of A, or three or more who are enemies of A. In former case suppose 'B, C and D' are friends of A. Any two of these individuals are friends, then these two with A form a group of 3 mutual friends. Otherwise, B, C and D are mutual enemies. Also by symmetry we can prove for the latter case of 'three or more who are enemies of A'.

39. **Answer:**   8

Logic for Solution: There are seven days of the week. Hence seven people can have birthdays on seven different days. We cannot guarantee that two of them must have the birthdays on the same day. Now if we take eighth person, he/she must have birthday on one of the overlapping day.

40. **Answer:** Now for any number (integer), it is divisible by zero if digit at one's place (digit on the right) is zero. The digit at one's place of the sum of two numbers is zero if sum of the digits at one's place of two numbers is 10. Digit at one's place of the difference of two numbers is zero if both digits at one's place of two numbers are equal. Thus sum or difference is divisible by 10 if and only if the digits at one's place of both numbers are same or they are one of the pairs, (0, 0), (1, 9), (2, 8), (3, 7), (4, 6) or (5, 5).

Let us make and label the pigeonholes for these numbers. First pigeonhole is for number zero, second pigeon hole is for number 1 and 9 to occupy and so on for (2, 8), (3, 7), (4, 6), and 5. Thus we have six pigeonholes for the numbers. Now if we take seven integers and consider the numbers at one's place as pigeons, there would be seven pigeons. These seven pigeons are to occupy six pigeonholes. Thus by pigeonhole principle there are at least two numbers (pigeons) in at least one pigeonhole. These numbers have same digit at one's place or have their sum as 10. Thus we have proved that at least one sum or difference of seven selected integers is divisible by 10.

41. **Answer:** Suppose that in a group $X = \{1, 2, ...,n\}$ there are k people who do not know anybody in the group. Now, consider three cases.

a) If $k > 1$, then there are at least two people who know zero people in the group. Hence, at least two people know same number (zero) of people in the group.

b) If $k = 0$. Let xi be the number of people known to i^{th} person where i = 1, 2, ...,n. Since there is no one who does not knows anybody (knows zero people in the group), and one could know maximum of (n – 1) people in a group of n people we get the condition that x_i satisfies is $1 \leq x_i \leq (n-1)$ for each i. Since there is n number of x_i and these can take any of only (n –1) values, by pigeonhole principle at least two values of xi must be equal (n pigeons and n –1 pigeonholes). So, there are at least two people who know same number of people.

c) If $k = 1$, we ignore the person who does not know anybody in the group. Now we have a group of remaining (n –1) people with $k = 0$. With similar arguments given in b) above, we prove the result.

Thus the result is true in general.

42. **Answer:** Now, let number of win for any player is i. From the given conditions, $1 \leq i \leq (n-1)$. We can consider that there are (n 1) numbers of possible wins as pigeonholes and n players as the pigeons. By pigeonhole principle, if n pigeons come to roost in n -1 pigeonhole, there would be at least one pigeonhole which has 2 or more pigeons. Thus, there would be at least two players who have exactly same number of wins.

To derive full benefit, do not refer to the answer unless you make enough efforts to solve the puzzle.

43. Answer: First, the man takes the goat across, leaving the wolf with the grass. Then he goes back. Next, he takes the wolf across. Then the man goes back, taking the goat with him. After this, he takes the grass across. Then he goes back again, leaving the wolf with the grass. Finally, he takes the goat across. We can also get another solution little differently. The principle is simple. Either take goat or wolf him while going across or returning. Only time he can take grass with him when wolf and goat are on two different banks of the river.

Logic for Solution: Here the Goat is common factor. Hence goat must be kept alone on any of the bank or man must accompany it. Thus the man must take goat first. Also when wolf and grass are there on two banks, man must travel with goat. Rest is simple.

44. Answer: For solving this problem we consider three cases.

Case I

There is no person who is without a friend i.e. zero friends. Thus everyone has number of friends ranging from 1 to 19. Obviously since these are total 20 people one cannot have more than 19 friends. Let ai be number of friends, i^{th} person has. Now, $1 \le a_i \le 19$, where i is from 1 to 20. Thus there are 20 numbers whose values are between 1 and 19. Number 1 to 19 can be considered as pigeonholes i.e. $n = 19$ and numbers ai as pigeons which is $20 = n + 1$. Thus there is at least one pigeonhole that has two or more pigeons in it. Thus $a_i = a_j$ for some i and j. Thus ith and j^{th} persons have same number of friends.

Case II

There is one person with no friends (zero friends). Hence all other 19 people can have friends from 1 to 18. Thus pigeon holes are number 1 to 18, total $n = 18$. Number of pigeons is 19. Hence by pigeonhole principle there must be at least two people who have same number of friends.

Case III

Two or more people have no friend (zero friends). In this case these are the two people who have same number of friend viz. zero.

Thus we have proved the result for all the cases.

45. Answer: Let the selected 101 number be expressed as, $X_i = 2^k \times a_i$ such that a_i is an odd number, for $i = 1, 2, \ldots 101$.

e.g $1 = 2^0 \times 1$ $2 = 2^1 \times 1$ $3 = 2^0 \times 3$ $4 = 2^2 \times 1$
$5 = 2^0 \times 5$ $6 = 2^1 \times 3$ $7 = 2^0 \times 7$ $8 = 2^3$
$9 = 2^0 \times 9$ $10 = 2^1 \times 5$ $11 = 2^0 \times 11$ $12 = 2^2 \times 3$
etc.

Since the numbers x_i which are expressed as are selected from 1 to 200, a_i 200. Also as per our definition a_i is odd. Since these are 101 numbers selected, there are 101 odd numbers a_i.

Now, there are in all 100 odd numbers from 1 to 200. If we consider these 100 odd numbers between the numbers 1 to 200 as pigeonholes and 101 odd numbers a_i as pigeons, by pigeonhole principle there at least two of the a_i are equal. If these numbers are say, i^{th} and j^{th} numbers, then $a_j = a_i$. Now if we divide larger number by small, as say $\frac{x_j}{x_i} = \frac{2^{k_j} \times a_i}{2^{k_i} \times a_i} = 2^n$. Since k_i and k_j are integers and $k_j > k_i$ hence $n = (k_j - k_i)$ is an integer. Therefore 2^n is also an integer. Thus one number divides other.

46. Answer: 11 Keys of each room.

Logic for Solution: Now we need to distribute keys to 100 ML As such that if we select any 90 ML As they must have keys of 90 rooms. In other words even if 10 ML As are absent the keys that they hold should also be with someone else. Since we are going to leave any 10 ML As this implies we must have minimum of 11 keys of each room. These keys must be distributed such ways that there is no commonality of keys held by any ML As. Hence after removing any 10 ML As remaining ML As must have key for each room. The way keys must be distributed is as follows. Let us name 100 MLAs $m_1, m_2, m_3, \ldots, m_{100}$ and number the keys of the 90 rooms as $k_1, k_2, k_3, \ldots, k_{90}$. Now we give keys of room number one i.e. k_1 to MLA m1 to m11. Keys of room number two i.e. k_2 to MLAs m_2 to m_{12} and so on till, we give room 90 key i.e. k_{90} to MLAs m_{90} to m100.

Now MLAs m1 to m i -1 will open the rooms 1 to i-1 room if i^{th} MLA m_i is the first MLA absent. In that case MLA m_{i+1} will open room number i and this continues till MLA m_{j-1} who will open room number j – 2. If MLA m_j is the next MLA absent, MLA m_{j+1} will open room number j-1 and so on.

47. **Answer:** Let us make pigeonholes for two consecutive address numbers, like 1000&1001, 1001&1002, etc. This way we have 99 pigeonholes for the numbers between 1000 and 1099. Now 51 houses as pigeons can be given any of the numbers where they can occupy the pigeonholes. But since except numbers 1000 and 1099 all are labeled twice, every house bearing those numbers would occupy two pigeon holes simultaneously. Only two houses numbered 1000 and 1099 would occupy only one pigeonhole. Thus there are 2 + 49 X 2 = 100 pigeons. Now, with 99 pigeonholes and 100 pigeons, using pigeonhole principle, we conclude that there would be at least one pigeonhole which has two pigeons. In other words at least two houses have consecutive numbers as addresses. Hence we proved the result.

48. **Answer:** i) Two wheelers 192, Three wheeler 1, Four wheelers 57

    Or ii) Two wheelers 191, Three wheelers 3, Four wheelers 56

    Or iii) Two wheelers 190, Three wheelers 5, Four wheelers 55

Logic for Solution: Let x, y and z the variables for number of two wheelers, three wheelers and four wheelers respectively. From given information we can right equations as,

$$2x+3y+4z=615 \text{ and } x+y+z=250$$

Solving we get, $z = \frac{115-y}{2}$

Now z must be integer. Hence y must be odd integer. But maximum value of y is 5. So, we put values of y as 1, 3 and 5. Substituting we get the answers.

49. Answer: The statement is "I will be roasted."

Logic for Solution: The statement should be perpetual opposite of the punishment. So the king can never decide. Say, if king says that the statement is False. He has to roast him as a punishment. But then the statement becomes true. For the True statement punishment is to cut and eat raw. But then the statement becomes False. So the punishment is to roast him. But then the statement becomes true. So king cannot decide as the process perpetuate. So king has no choice but to let him free.

50. Answer:

a) If average of n positive numbers is t, then by definition of average sum of these n numbers is equal to $n \times t$. Suppose there is no number which is greater than or equal to t, it implies each number is less than t. Hence adding n numbers that are less than t we would get the sum of all numbers as less than $n \times t$. But this cannot be true because it is given that sum of all numbers is equal to $n \times t$. This implies that our hypothesis that no number which is greater than or equal to t is false. Hence there is at least one of the numbers is greater than or equal to t.

b) Similar arguments would prove that at least one of them is less than or equal to t.

51. Answer: The man goes to any one of the guard and asks, "If I had asked other the guard, whether this gate would take me to Gallows, what answer he would give." If the answer he gets 'Yes', he exits from this gate. If the answer is 'No', he would exit from the other gate.

Logic for Solution: One person always tells lie and other always truth. So we need to design a question which would consider both together. Now one lie plus one truth always makes a lie, so irrespective of who is the guard that you select for asking the question the answer is always a lie.

52. Answer: Sachin Tendulkar does not have Hummer at all.

Logic for Solution: Take a look at the statements about the number of 'Hummers' with Sachin Tendulkar. If Sourabh would be right ("at least four"), then Pushkar ("at least one") would also be right. If Pushkar would be right ("at least one"), then or Sourabh ("at least four") or Shirish ("less than four") would also be right. So this means only Shirish can be right and with less than one 'Hummers' with Sachin Tendulkar. So the only possible answer is 'there is no Hummer with Sachin Tendulkar at all'.

53. Answer: After 19 days.

Logic for Solution: The water-lily doubles in size every day. So the size on the 20th day will be double that of 19th day. After exactly 20 days the complete pool will be covered by the lily. So after 19 days half pool will be covered.

54. Answer: You should turn the cards with the 'A' and the '9'.

Logic for Solution: The 'A' should be turned to verify that there is an even digit on the other side. When there is an odd digit on the other side, the statement is not true. Then '9' should be turned to verify that there is no vowel on the other side. When there is a vowel on the other side, the statement is not true.

Note that statement to be proved is "When there is a vowel on one side of a card, there is an even digit on the other side". It does not state what should be on the other side of consonant. It also does not state that a vowel has to be there on the other side of an even number. So we won't get any useful information by turning the 'B' or the '6'. After all, it is not stated that only cards with a vowel have an even digit on the other side!

55. Answer: Sheetal could ask Parag "I have the number 1 or 2 in my mind. Is the number that you have in mind greater than the number I have in mind?"

Logic for Solution: If the answer is "yes" means that Parag has number 3 in mind, because it is greater than both 1 and 2. If the answer is "I can't say" means Parag has number 2 in his mind and he cannot give answer; the answer would be "yes" or "no" depending upon the number Sheetal has in mind and Parag does not know it. If the answer is "no" means Parag has number 1 in mind. Since there are three numbers we must design a question related to three numbers that has three answers depending upon the number in Parag's mind. Three answers could be 'Yes', 'No' and 'Can't Say'. Once you understand this logic, designing the question is easy.

Note: If there is no condition of the type of answers, then things would be easy. Sheetal could just ask "Is your number greater than two or less than two?" Of course Sheetal could directly ask "Tell me what is your number?" Well that's just a fun and not logic!!

56. Answer: First mark the switches as 1, 2, and 3. Then put on the switch 1 for a few minutes. Then turn off the switch 1 and turn on the switch 2. Now enter the room. If the light bulb is lit, then it is clear that switch 2 is connected to it. If the bulb is not lit, then it has to be switch 1 or 3. Now touch the light bulb and check its temperature. If the bulb is hot, means it was 'ON' just some time ago. Hence the switch 1 is connected to the bulb. Whereas, if the bulb is cold, then it has to be connected to the switch 3.

Logic for Solution: Since there are three switches, we have made three possible states using the fact that light bulb becomes hot if switched 'ON' and it takes time to cool down after it is switched 'OFF'. Thus the three states are 'ON', 'OFF and Hot' and 'OFF and Cold'

57. Answer: The suspect B is a thief.

Logic for Solution: It follows from the introduction that statement A3 is true. Now we can count how many of the remaining statements are true or false. If the statement could either be true or false we write accordingly. The statement wise analysis is given below for various situations viz. A or B or C or D or Somebody Else is the thief of the car:

Statement Number	Possible Car Thief				
	A	B	C	D	
A1	True / False	True / False	True / False	True / False	True / False
A2	True / False	True / False	True / False	True / False	True / False
A3	True	True	True	True	True
B1	False	False	True	False	False
B2	False	True	True	True	True
B3	True / False	True / False	True / False	True / False	True / False
C1	True / False	True / False	True / False	True / False	True / False
C2	True	False	True	True	True
C3	False	False	False	True	False
D1	True	True	False	True	True
D2	True	True	True	False	True
D3	True	False	False	False	False
Total	5 True +	4 True +	5 True +	5 True +	5 True +

The True is written when the statement is true if the corresponding suspect is indeed a thief. For example the statement B1 'Suspect C is the guilty one' is 'True' only if suspect C has stolen the car. If anyone other than C has stolen the car, the statement B1 would be 'False'. The False is written when the statement is 'False' if the corresponding suspect is indeed a thief. For example the statement C2 'Suspect B is innocent' is 'False' only if suspect B has stolen the car. If anyone other than B has stolen the car, the statement C2 would be 'True'. Also some of the statements could be 'True/False' irrespective of who is the thief.

Now there are only four statements are 'True'. As can be seen from the total it is possible only when suspect B is the offender. Also all the 'True/False' statements are False. Hence suspect B must be thief.

58. **Answer:** Deepak had his own coat, Prasanna's hat, Parag's gloves, and Nachiket's cane. Prasanna had his own coat, Nachiket's hat, Deepak's gloves, and Parag's cane. Parag had Nachiket's coat, his own hat, Prasanna's gloves, and Deepak's cane. Nachiket had Parag's coat, Deepak's hat, his own gloves, and Prasanna's cane.

Logic for the Solution: Let us start making a matrix and fill it with the available information.

	Deepak	Prasanna	Parag	Nachiket
Coat	Deepak's	Prasanna's	Nachiket's	Parag's
Hat	Prasanna's	Nachiket's	Parag's	Deepak's
Gloves	Parag's	Deepak's	Prasanna's	Nachiket's
Cane	Nachiket's	Parag's	Deepak's	Prasanna's

The steps are given below. The information is extracted from the puzzle and entered in the tale.

a) Each of the men ended up with exactly one article of clothing belonging to each one of the four.

b) Deepak and Prasanna ended up with their own coats, Parag ended up with his own hat, and Nachiket ended up with his own gloves. Enter it in table.

c) Deepak did not end up with Parag's cane. But Deepak cannot have Parags's Hat as Parag has it. Also Deepak cannot have Parag's coat as Deepak already has own coat. So to satisfy the statement a) Deepak must have Parag's gloves. Fill this in the table.

d) Now consider the gloves. Parag's and Nachiket's gloves are already accounted. Hence to satisfy the statement a) Prasanna can have only Deepak's gloves. Obviously now Parag can only have Prasanna's gloves. Fill this information in the table.

e) Now consider the coat. To satisfy statement a) and b) Parag can only have Nachiket's coat and Nachiket can only have Parag's. Fill this information in the table.

f) Now in case of Parag, he can have only cane of Deepak to satisfy statement a). Fill this information in the table.

g) Now Deepak's hat can only be with Nachiket to satisfy statement a). Fill this information in the table.

h) Obviously now Nachiket has Prasanna's cane. Fill this information in the table.

i) Now we can see that Prasanna can only have Parag's cane. Then Nachiket's hat. Fill this information in the table.

j) Finally we can fill remaining cells with Deepak having Prasanna's hat and Nachiket's cane. Fill this information in the table and we got the answer.

59. Answer: Pournima's husband is Deepak.

Logic for Solution: From the second statement b), we know that the six people sat at the table in the following way (anticlockwise and starting with Pournima's husband):

'Sheetal, man, woman, man, woman, Pournima's husband'

The last statement d) states Pournima did not sit beside her husband, hence the situation must be as follows:

'Sheetal, man, Pournima, man, woman, Pournima's husband'

The remaining woman must be Pranita, hence the situation becomes:

'Sheetal, man, Pournima, man, Pranita, Pournima's husband'

With the first statement a), we arrive at the following situation:

To derive full benefit, do not refer to the answer unless you make enough efforts to solve the puzzle.

'Sheetal, Prasanna, Pournima, man, Pranita, Pournima's husband'

As per the third statement c), Parag and Deepak can be placed in only one way, and we now know the complete order as follows:

'Sheetal, Prasanna, Pournima, Parag, Pranita, Deepak (Pournima's husband)'

Thus we conclude: the name of Pournima's husband's name is Deepak.

60. Answer: Suhas's wife shook 4 hands.

Logic for Solution: Because, obviously, no person shook hands with himself or herself, or with his or her partner (I am sure they were acquainted with), hence nobody could have shaken hands with more than eight other people. And since nine people shook hands with different numbers of people, these numbers must be 0, 1, 2, 3, 4, 5, 6, 7, and 8.

The person, who shook 8 hands, shook hands with all other persons, except with his or her spouse. Hence all people other than his or her spouse shook hands with at least one person. Therefore, the partner of the person who shook 8 hands must be the person who shook 0 hands.

The person who shook 7 hands, shook hands with all other persons, except with his or her spouse and the person who shook 0 hands as identified earlier. Hence all persons other than his or her spouse and the person who shook exactly 0 hands, must have shaken at least 2 hands. Therefore, the spouse of the person who shook 7 hands, must be the person who shook 1 hand.

Continuing with similar arguments, the spouse of the person who shook 6 hands would have shaken 2 hands. Also the spouse of the person who shook 5 hands would have shaken 3 hands.

The only person left is the one who shook 4 hands, and which must be Suhas's wife. Hence, Suhas's wife shook 4 hands.

To derive full benefit, do not refer to the answer unless you make enough efforts to solve the puzzle.

61. Answer: Take a piece of fruit from the box with the labels 'Apples and Mangos'. It will be either an Apple or a Mango. 'Apples and Mangos' label is known to be wrong, hence remove it. Whatever the fruit is the box having the label by that name remove it and put it on the first box. Then remove the label from the third box and put it on the second box. The label 'Apples and Mangos' is for the third box.

Logic for Solution: Take a piece of fruit from the box with the labels 'Apples and Mangos'. If it is an apple, then the correct label should have been either 'Apples' or 'Apples and Mangos'. But since no label is put correctly, 'Apples and Mangos' label is wrong. Hence the correct label for this box must be 'Apples'. Now we are left with two boxes. The box that has a label 'Apples' cannot have a label 'Apples and Mangos' because in that case the third box label 'Mangoes' was correct, which is contrary to the given condition that all the labels are put wrongly. Hence the box with label 'Apples', must have the correct label as 'Mangos'. On the last box with the label 'Mangos' should have the label 'Apples and Mangos'.

Suppose the fruit you have taken from the box labeled 'Apples and Mangos' is a 'Mango', the reasoning would be similar to find the correct labels for all the boxes.

62. Answer: No, it is not possible to cut the chess-board paper into pieces such that each piece has twice as much squares of one color than of the other color.

Proof: If it is possible, then every piece would have a number of squares divisible by 3 (because if a piece has n squares of one color and 2×n squares of the other color, it has 3×n squares in total). The total number of squares of all pieces would then also be divisible by 3. This is, however, impossible since the total number of squares on the chess-board is 64, which is not divisible by 3.

63. Answer: The day on which Santa Singh tells the truth is Tuesday.

Logic for Solution: We know that Santa Singh tells the truth on only a single day of the week.

Now on day 1 he may be telling Truth or telling lie. If he is telling truth he lies on Monday and Tuesday. Or if the statement on day 1 is a lie, this means that he tells the truth on either Monday or Tuesday.

On day 2 he may be telling Truth or telling lie. If he is telling truth day 2 is Thursday, Saturday, or Sunday. Or if the statement on day 2 is a lie, this means day 2 is Monday, Tuesday, Wednesday or Friday.

If the statement on day 3 is true he lies on Wednesday and Friday. If it is a lie, this means that he tells the truth on either Wednesday or Friday.

Now since Santa Singh tells the truth on only one day, then at the most only one of these statements could be true and other two or all three statements must be lies. Let us check if any lies cannot coexist.

Day 1 lie implies he tells truth on either Monday or Tuesday. Day 2 lie implies the day 2 is Monday, Tuesday, Wednesday or Friday. Day 3 lie implies he tells truth on either Wednesday or Friday. There is no contradiction in Day1 and Day 2 being lies. Similarly there is no contradiction in Day3 and Day 2 being lies. However Day 1 and Day 3 can't be lies together because in that case he tells truth on Monday or Tuesday and also tells truth on Wednesday or Friday. This is not possible as he speaks truth only on one day. Thus out of the statements on Day 1 and Day 2, one has to be true and other lie.

Assume that the statement on day 1 is true. Then the statement on day 3 must be untrue, from which follows that Santa Singh tells the truth on Wednesday or Friday. So, day 1 is a Wednesday or a Friday. Therefore, day 2 is a Thursday or a Saturday. However, this would imply that the statement on day 2 is true, which is impossible. From this we can conclude that the statement on day 1 must be lie. This means that Santa Singh told the truth on day 3 and hence the day 3 is a Monday or a Tuesday. So day 2 is a Sunday or a Monday. Because the statement on day 2 must be a lie, we can conclude that day 2 is a Monday.

So day 3 is a Tuesday. Therefore, the day on which Santa Singh tells the truth is Tuesday.

64. Answer: No, you cannot fill the board.

Proof: Chess-board has alternative white and black squares. Thus we have equal number of white and black squares. Diagonally opposite corners are of the same colours. Hence removing diagonally opposite squares would make number of white and number of black squares unequal. Each brick will cover two adjacent squares that is one white and one black square of the board. So the number of bricks equals the number of white squares equals the number of black squares. Hence to cover the board with bricks as per the rules will not be possible as the bricks cover equal number of white and black squares whereas we have unequal number of white and black squares.

65. Answer: Yes.

Logic for Solution: Consider all three police officers and prisoners are on one bank, say Bank1. Now we will explain the forward and return trips. Also we will indicate how many police officers and prisoners are there on each bank during and after the trip.

The diagrammatic display of the situation as per the movement is given below:

% indicates Police officer, + indicates Prisoner and * indicates Prisoner who knows operating the boat.

Step	Status	Bank 1 Position	Boat occupation	Bank 2 Position
1	Start	%, %, %, *, +, +		
2	Boat moving from Bank 1 to Bank 2	%, %, %, +	*, +	
3	Boat reaches Bank 2	%, %, %, +		*, +
4	Boat moving from Bank 2 to Bank 1	%, %, %, +	*	+
5	Boat reaches Bank 1	%, %, %, +, *		+
6	Boat moving from Bank 1 to Bank 2	%, %, %	+, *	+
7	Boat reaches Bank 2	%, %, %		+, +, *
8	Boat moving from Bank 2 to Bank 1	%, %, %	*	+, +
9	Boat reaches Bank 1	%, %, %, *		+, +
10	Boat moving from Bank 1 to Bank 2	%, *	%, %	+, +
11	Boat reaches Bank 2	%, *		%, %, +, +
12	Boat moving from Bank 2 to Bank 1	%, *	%, +	%, +
13	Boat reaches Bank 1	%, %, *, +		%, +
14	Boat moving from Bank 1 to Bank 2	%, +	%, *	%, +
15	Boat reaches Bank 2	%, +		%, %, *, +
16	Boat moving from Bank 2 to Bank 1	%, +	%, +	%, *

To derive full benefit, do not refer to the answer unless you make enough efforts to solve the puzzle.

17	Boat reaches Bank 1	%, %, +, +			%, *
18	Boat moving from Bank 1 to Bank 2	+, +	%, %		%, *
19	Boat reaches Bank 2	+, +			%, %, %, *
20	Boat moving from Bank 2 to Bank 1	+, +		*	%, %, %
21	Boat reaches Bank 1	+, +, *			%, %, %
22	Boat moving from Bank 1 to Bank 2	+		+, *	%, %, %
23	Boat reaches Bank 2	+			%, %, %, +, *
24	Boat moving from Bank 2 to Bank 1	+		*	%, %, %, +
25	Boat reaches Bank 1	+, *			%, %, %, +
26	Boat moving from Bank 1 to Bank 2			+, *	%, %, %, +
27	Boat reaches Bank 2				%, %, %, *, +, +

Please note that the steps 15 to 27 are the mirror images of steps 1 to 13 and the step 14 is one Police officer and one Prisoner on each side and one Police officer and Prisoner who knows operating the boat are in the boat.

66. Answer: There's the same amount of alcohol in the water as water in the alcohol.

Logic for the Solution: Each glass ends with the same volume of liquid that it started with. So, if 'x' ml of alcohol has gone in water, 'x' ml of water had come out from the glass of water and gone in the glass of alcohol.

67. Answer:

Professor Umesh Patwardhan teaches math and Law
Professor Anjali Vamburkar teaches Finance and Law
Professor Meghana Limaye teaches Finance and Economics
Professor Shailashree Haridas teaches Finance and Economics.

Logic for Solution: From statement e) Professor Umesh is only one who doesn't teach Finance. Whereas from statement a) there are three Professors who teach Finance implying all Professors except Professor Umesh teach Finance. Also from statement g) Professor Patwardhan doesn't teach any course that is taught by Professor Shailashree or Professor Limaye. It follows that Professor Umesh and Professor Patwardhan are the same person.

Now four Professors teach two subjects each. Thus there are 4 X 2 = 8 teacher subject combinations. From statement a) three combinations are of Finance, from statement b) only one combination is of Math and from statement c) two are of Law. Thus there are only two Professors who teach Economics. Obviously from statement d) Professor Umesh Patwardhan does not teach Economics. Hence he teaches Math and Law.

Now Professor Anjali teaches Law and Finance. From statement d) she cannot be Professor Haridas. Since Professor Anjali teaches same subject as Professor Patwardhan viz. Law, from statement g) she cannot be Professor Limaye. Hence Professor Anjali must be Professor Anjali Vamburkar.

Since Professor Shailashree and Professor Limaye are two different persons, just like Professor Meghana and Professor Haridas, the names of the other two Professors are Professor ShailashreeHaridas and Professor Meghana Limaye.

Thus, we get the answer.

To derive full benefit, do not refer to the answer unless you make enough efforts to solve the puzzle.

68. Answer: Sandhya made the seventh, winning move!

Logic for Solution: If Poorwa had made the sixth move with O, there are three possibilities for the situation after five moves:

Possibility 1   Possibility 2   Possibility 3

O		
O	X	
X	X	

	O	
O	X	
X	X	

O	O	
	X	
X	X	

In case of possibility 2 and 3 there is no reason for Poorwa to put the O at top left corner. It was neither completing row nor blocking opponent. She had a move to block the opponent with O in top right or bottom right corner. Hence only possibility 1 is correct.

If after fifth move by Sourabh had resulted in the possibility 1, there are three possibilities for the situation after four moves:

Possibility 1   Possibility 2   Possibility 3

O		
O	X	
	X	

	O	
O		
X	X	

O	O	
	X	
X		

In all the three cases Sourabh would have put a cross to complete a row and win the game. But since he did not win the game in fifth move implies that our assumption of Poorwa made the sixth move is incorrect. Thus the sixth move must have been made by Sourabh.

Now Sandhya can make the seventh, winning move!

Let us check that Sourabh had indeed made the sixth move. There are following three possibilities after fifth move by Poorwa:

Possibility 1

O	O	
O		
X	X	

Possibility 2

O	O	
O	X	
X		

Possibility 3

O	O	
O	X	
	X	

In case of possibility 1 and possibility 2 Sourabh would have completed the row and won the game. Since he did not complete the game implies that after fifth move the situation was that of possibility 3. This also justifies the sixth move in which he could have blocked Poorwa by putting cross X in cell bottom left or top right corner. He actually selected bottom left corner. This is perfectly possible.

69. **Answer:** The steps to get the solution are given below:
   a) Engine moves to stop 2-3 and then move on segment 2. Then it connects wagon B.
   b) Engine pulls wagon B to stop 2-3 and then pushes to the stop 1-3. Then it disconnects wagon B.
   c) Engine moves on segment 3 to stop 2-3. Then it moves on segment 2 to large junction merge of 1-2. Then it moves on segment 1 and pushes the wagon A to junction 1-3 till the wagon B.
   d) Wagons are connected and engine pulls both wagons on large junction of segment 1 and 2. Engine is connected to wagon A to which wagon B is connected.
   e) Then engine pushes both wagons till wagon B comes on the segment 2. Then it disconnects wagons A and B. Engine then pulls wagon A leaving wagon B on segment 2.
   h) Engine pushes wagon A on segment 1 till stop 1-3 on junction. Engine is disconnected and moves to the large junction of segments 1 and 2.
   i) Engine moves on segment 2, connects wagon B and pulls it to the large junction of segments 1 and 2. Then it pushes the wagon B on segment 1.

To derive full benefit, do not refer to the answer unless you make enough efforts to solve the puzzle.

j) The engine disconnects the wagon B leaving it on segment 1 and moves to large junction, segment 2, stop 2-3 and then to segment 3.

k) Engine moves to wagon A on stop 1-3 and connects it. Then it pulls wagon A to stop 2-3.

l) Engine pushes the wagon A on segment 2. It disconnects the wagon leaving it on segment 2.

m) Engine moves back to stop 2-3 and then on segment 3.

n) Now Engine has come to original position on segment 3, wagon A is on segment 2 and wagon B is on segment 1. Thus we have arrived in a situation where the wagons have changed places and the locomotive is back in its starting position.

70. **Answer:** First, label the containers of all the batches from 1 to 8. Now take one ball from the first batch, two balls from the second batch, three balls from the third batch, five balls from fourth batch, eight balls from fifth batch, 13 balls from sixth batch, 21 balls from seventh batch and 30 balls from eighth batch. Now weigh all the selected balls. If all the batches were without defect with all balls weighing 10 gm each, the total weight would have been, 10×1275=12750 gms

However, two of the batches have defective balls with weight of each ball is heavier by 0.2 gm. Thus the total weight is more by the amount depending upon the sum of number of balls selected from those defective batches multiplied by 0.2. Hence from the total weight of selected balls in grams, subtract 12750 divide the answer by 0.2. The resulting number is then split in two parts such that the two numbers are from 1, 2, 3, 5, 8, 13, 21 and 30. These numbers would give the batch number which has defective balls.

Logic for Solution: You need to elect the numbers such that sum of any two pairs should be equal. Because if they are equal then we will not be able to find which pair is defective.

For example if we select 1, 2, 3, 4, etc. and number of defective balls is 5. We cannot determine whether the batches 1 and 4 are defective or batches 2 and 3. Of course the answer is not unique. We could find different combination of numbers.

71. Answer: Consider all people are on one bank, say Bank 1. Now we will explain the forward and return trips. Also we will indicate who the people on each bank are during and after the trip. The diagrammatic display of the situation as per the movement is given below:

P indicates Police officer, T indicates Thief, F indicates Father, M indicates mother, B indicates Boy and G indicates Girl.

Step	Status	Position on Bank 1	In Boat	Position on Bank 2
1	Start	P, T, F, M, B, B, G, G		
2	Boat moving from Bank 1 to Bank 2	F, M, B, B, G, G	P, T	
3	Boat reaches Bank 2	F, M, B, B, G, G		P, T
4	Boat moving from Bank 2 to Bank 1	F, M, B, B, G, G	P	T
5	Boat reaches Bank 1	F, M, B, B, G, G, P		T
6	Boat moving from Bank 1 to Bank 2	F, M, B, G, G	P, B	T
7	Boat reaches Bank 2	F, M, B, G, G		T, P, B
8	Boat moving from Bank 2 to Bank 1	F, M, B, G, G	P, T	B
9	Boat reaches Bank 1	F, M, B, G, G, P, T		B

To derive full benefit, do not refer to the answer unless you make enough efforts to solve the puzzle.

10	Boat moving from Bank 1 to Bank 2	M, G, G, P, T	F, B	B
11	Boat reaches Bank 2	M, G, G, P, T		F, B, B
12	Boat moving from Bank 2 to Bank 1	M, G, G, P, T	F	B, B
13	Boat reaches Bank 1	M, G, G, P, T, F		B, B
14	Boat moving from Bank 1 to Bank 2	G, G, P, T	F, M	B, B
15	Boat reaches Bank 2	G, G, P, T		F, M, B, B
16	Boat moving from Bank 2 to Bank 1	G, G, P, T	M	F, B, B
17	Boat reaches Bank 1	G, G, P, T, M		F, B, B
18	Boat moving from Bank 1 to Bank 2	G, G, M	P, T	F, B, B
19	Boat reaches Bank 2	G, G, M		P, T, F, B, B
20	Boat moving from Bank 2 to Bank 1	G, G, M	F	P, T, B, B
21	Boat reaches Bank 1	G, G, M, F		P, T, B, B
22	Boat moving from Bank 1 to Bank 2	G, G	M, F	P, T, B, B
23	Boat reaches Bank 2	G, G		P, T, B, B, M, F
24	Boat moving from Bank 2 to Bank 1	G, G	M	P, T, B, B, F
25	Boat reaches Bank 1	G, G, M		P, T, B, B, F
26	Boat moving from Bank 1 to Bank 2	G	G, M	P, T, B, B, F

To derive full benefit, do not refer to the answer unless you make enough efforts to solve the puzzle.

27	Boat reaches Bank 2	G		P, T, B, B, F, G, M
28	Boat moving from Bank 2 to Bank 1	G	P, T	B, B, F, G, M
29	Boat reaches Bank 1	G, P, T		B, B, F, G, M
30	Boat moving from Bank 1 to Bank 2	T	P, G	B, B, F, G, M
31	Boat reaches Bank 2	T		P, B, B, F, G, M
32	Boat moving from Bank 2 to Bank 1	T	P	B, B, F, G, M
33	Boat reaches Bank 1	P, T		B, B, F, G, M
34	Boat moving from Bank 1 to Bank 2		P, T	B, B, F, G, M
35	Boat reaches Bank 2			P, T, B, B, F, G, G, M

Please note that the steps 19 to 35 are the mirror images of steps 1 to 17 and the step 18 is symmetric.

72. **Answer:** 19 horses were distributed as, elder got 10 horses, younger got 5 and youngest got 4.

Logic for Solution: Quick calculations tells us that the proportion distributed as,

1/2 + 1/4 +1/5 = 19/20 Thus rather that 1 the distribution is 19/20 and 1/20 portion is left out. The denominator 20 indicates we need one more horse to distribute and after distribution 1 horse will be left out. This leads to the answer.

73. **Answer:** First the army unit commander sends the secret plan in the box after putting two locks on the box so that the plan reaches field officer safely. The commander retains the keys for both the locks. Then the field officer puts his two locks, retains the keys and sends the box

back to the commander. Now commander removes two locks that he had put and sends the box again. Finally when the box reaches the field officer, he can now remove the locks and take out the secret plan safely.

Logic for Solution: The intelligent man riding on the horse added his horse to the 19 horses making total 20. Then he gave half of 20 i.e. 10 to the elder brother. Then he gave quarter of 20 i.e. 5 to the younger brother. Finally he gave one fifth of 20 i.e. 4 to the youngest brother. Then of course he took the remaining horse which was his, and continued his journey.

74. **Answer:** The daughter puts hand in the bag, picks one pebble and quickly drops it on ground (or throws it away). She then tells the villagers to check the remaining pebble in the bag. Obviously it would be a black. This implies the pebble that she had picked was white. So the farmer gets loan waiver and the farmer's daughter doesn't have to marry the old ugly money lender!

75. **Answer:** 192

Logic for Solution: First keep 7 trays with water in alternate trays and trays in between are kept upside down (empty). Thus four trays would have water including bottom and top trays. In ten minutes we would get 4×12=48 ice cubes. Now stack all seven trays with full water with two ice cubes in diagonally opposite corners in each tray except top tray. (These cubes are from the ones made in first lot). Now in next ten minutes we would get additional 7×12-12= 72 ice cubes. Also in the third round we would get 72 ice cubes. Hence in 30 minutes we get maximum of 192 ice cubes.

76. **Answer:** His son.

77. Square manhole cover can drop inside since diagonal of the manhole is larger than the side. Whereas circular cover can never drop in side.

To derive full benefit, do not refer to the answer unless you make enough efforts to solve the puzzle.

78. Answer: First mark the switches as 1, 2, 3 and 4. Then put on the switch 1 for a long time. Then turn off the switch 1 and turn on the switch 2 for few minutes. Now turn on the switch 3 without switching off the position of the switch 2. Immediately enter the room, observe the light and also touch the light to check its temperature. If the light is lit, and cold then it is clear that switch 3 is controls the light. If the light is lit, and hot then it is clear that switch 2 is controlling the light. If the light is not lit, but hot means it was 'ON' just some time ago, then the switch 1 controls the light. Whereas, if the light is not lit and cold, then the switch 4 controls the light.

Logic for Solution: Since we had four switches we must identify four states. Here we have made three states using the fact that light bulb becomes hot if switched 'ON' and it takes time to cool down after it is switched 'OFF'. Thus we created four states 'ON & Hot', 'ON & Cold', 'OFF & Hot' and OFF & Cold'. Now relate these to the switch positions and we get the answer. This is similar to the puzzle 58 with one more state included.

79. Answer: He told them to ride each other's camels.

Logic for Solution: Role reversal changes situation reverse.

80. Answer: India came in first. Sri Lanka and South Africa tied for second place. Pakistan came in fourth. Australia came fifth.

Logic for the Solution:

The statement a) tells the order 'India – Pakistan – Australia'.

Statement b) is conditional, so we consider it afterwards.

To satisfy statement c) Sri Lanka must be between India and Pakistan. So the situation is as follows.

'India – Sri Lanka – Pakistan – Australia'.

Now South Africa can be put at one of the positions shown by dashes. We know that India can not be tied with Pakistan or else condition c) is violated. Therefore from the condition b) South Africa is tied with Sri Lanka. This also satisfies the condition c).

81. **Answer:** First surgeon performs the operation by wearing two gloves on right hand, one on the top of other. Let us call inner glove as A and outer glove as B. Thus the outer side of the glove B (outer glove) gets exposed to the driver's blood and inner side of the glove A gets exposed to first doctor's blood. Now first doctor with left hand (which does not have any exposed wound) removes the glove B. Second surgeon now puts on the glove B which has clean inner side and performs the operation. With this the glove B gets exposed from inner side to second surgeon's blood. From outer side it was in any case exposed to the driver's blood, so there was no problem during operation of exposing again. Then first surgeon with left hand removes the glove A while reversing. Thus the clean outer side of glove A. now becomes inner side. Now third surgeon puts on the reversed glove A whose outer side is exposed to the blood of the first surgeon. He further puts glove B (without reversing it) on the top of the glove A. Now he performs the operation. With this the glove A gets exposed from reversed inner side (original outer side) to third surgeon's blood. The glove B outer side that was in any case exposed to the driver's blood, and so won't make any difference during operation.

Logic for Solution: There are four people involved who do not want to expose to each other's blood. There are two gloves that have four surfaces. So the gloves must be put on such that each one is exposed only to one side.

82. **Answer:** Rs 10 did not go anywhere.

Logic for Solution: It is just an incorrect way to look at the expenditure out of Rs 300 that three friends had. The friends amongst themselves spent Rs 270, out of which Rs 250 was the bill amount and Rs 20 was the tip. So 250 + 20 makes 270.

83. **Answer:** Let us track the quantity of water in jugs as 12 liter jug/8 liter jug/5 liter jug. First pour the water from 12 liter jug to fill 8 liter jug. The situation is 4/8/0. Now pour the water from 8 liter jug to fill 5 liter jug. The situation is 4/3/5. Now empty the 5 liter jug in 12 liter jug. The position is 9/3/0. Now empty the content of 8 liter jug in 5 liter jug. The position is 9/0/3. Then pour the water from 12 liter jug to fill 8 liter jug. The position is 1/8/3. Now fill 5 liter jug from 8 liter jug. The position is 1/6/5. Finally pour the water from 5 liter jug to 12 liter jug. The final situation is 6/6/0. Thus is the answer.

84. **Answer:** Yes, you should change since probability of finding the gift is now 2/3 i.e. 0.67

Logic for Solution: Let us give numbers to the doors as 1, 2 and 3. Now let us consider that you have selected door 1. (Till now the steps are arbitrary and any door selection would have same logic and hence probability). Now the game host opens other door and shows there is no gift. Of course since he knows where the gift is he would not open the door where the gift is. Now consider the three possibilities.

a) Gift is behind the door 1: Irrespective of which door he opens, by changing the door you will lose the gift.

b) Gift is behind the door 2: Host would open door 3 and hence changing the door you will get the gift.

c) Gift is behind the door 3: Host would open door 2 and hence changing the door you will get the gift.

Note all the three possibilities considered above are equally likely. Out of three possible outcomes two are in your favour if you change the choice of the door. Hence probability of finding the gift by changing the door once he opens and shows empty door becomes 2/3. On the other hand probability of not finding the gift after changing the door is 1/3. Since the probability of finding the gift after changing the door is higher

To derive full benefit, do not refer to the answer unless you make enough efforts to solve the puzzle.

than not changing the door, you should change the door. (The confusion arises if you just use your common sense and knowledge of basics of probability because you ignore the fact that host knows where the gift is and hence does not open the door randomly as required by the probability theory).

85. Answer: The girl is born on 28th February on non-leap year just before midnight. The after few minutes (past midnight) her twin brother was born on 1st March. Now the present year is a leap year. So the girl celebrates her birthday on 28th February, then after one day gap on 29th February, the twin brother celebrated his birthday on 1st March i.e. after two days.

Logic for Solution: Day changes at Midnight. Leap year has one additional day. If we use both, then there is difference of dates by two.

86. Answer: Your spouse was acquainted with five people and you were also acquainted with five people.

Logic for Solution: Totally there are 10people. So any one can be acquainted with at the most 9 people (obviously one must leave himself or herself in the count) Also everybody knows their own spouses (hopefully). Hence everybody knew at least1 person. Other than you, everyone is acquainted with a different number of people. There are 9 people other than you. Let us name them for convenience A, B, C, D, E, F, G, H and I. That means number of people acquainted to the nine people other than you are 9, 8, 7, 6, 5, 4, 3, 2 and 1 respectively.

Now start with the person A, who is acquainted with 9 people, that is everybody else. Obviously all other than A's spouse are acquainted with A and their own spouse. Thus all other than A's spouse are acquainted with at least 2 people. Hence it must be A's spouse who is acquainted with exactly one person i.e. A. Thus A's spouse is person I. So we have identified persons with 1 and 9 acquaintances as husband and wife A and I. Now consider B who is acquainted with exactly 8 people. Person B knows everybody except for I who only knows his/her spouse. Person H is acquainted with 2 people. That has to

To derive full benefit, do not refer to the answer unless you make enough efforts to solve the puzzle.

be person B and person A. Person A is married to person I, so person H's spouse must be person B. Continuing with similar arguments, person C knows 7 people i.e. everybody except for persons I and H. Person G therefore knows C, B, and A. Persons B and A are married to persons H and I respectively. So person G's spouse must be person C. Further, with similar arguments person D must be the spouse of F.

This leaves person E, who knows everyone except persons I, H, G and F. These five people, therefore, must be persons A, B, C, D, and you. Since you are the only one of these five not yet paired up, person E must be your spouse. So your spouse knew five people prior to the tour.

The above also determines that the people you are acquainted are A, B, C, D and E. So you are also acquainted with exactly five people prior to the tour.

87. **Answer:** 3: You have 1 each of rose, tulip and carnation.
Alternative Answer: You have 2 two flowers other than roses, tulips and carnations. So other than these two, all means zero roses, tulips and carnations. (However, this answer is not a very convincing as all usually is not referred to zero)
Logic for the Solution: If you consider Y as total number of flowers, and X_1, X_2 and X_3 are number of roses, tulips and carnations, we can write statements as equations,
$Y-2=X_1$, $Y-2=X_2$, $Y-2=X_3$ and $Y=X_1+X_2+X_3$
Solving we get answer as $Y = 3$

88. **Answer:** Number the connector contacts on one surface clockwise, with consecutive numbers: 1, 2, 3, 4, 5, 6, 7. Number the other surface contacts clockwise, with every other number, then wrapping back around as: 1, 3, 5, 7, 2, 4, 6.
Alternate Answer: Number the connector contacts on one surface clockwise, with consecutive numbers: 1, 2, 3, 4, 5, 6, 7. Number the other surface contacts clockwise, with every other number, then wrapping back around as: 1, 5, 2, 6, 3, 7, 4.

Logic for the Solution: First we mark the contacts on one surface as 1, 2, 3, 4, 5, 6 and 7. Now any one contact on the other surface must match. Let contact 1 match with 1. Now rotate the contactor clockwise through one seventh revolution so that output side is rotated through one step. Now second contact of output side is shifted through one step and is aligned with number 3 (2+1) of input side. Hence this second point of output side should be numbered 3. Now again rotate the contactor clockwise through one seventh revolution so that output side is rotated through one step. Now third contact of output side is shifted through two steps and is aligned with number 5 (3+2) of input side. Hence this third point of output side should be numbered 5. Similarly with next rotation step the output connector is aligned with number 7 of input side. Continuing in same way the next output contact will be aligned with 2 then 4 and finally 6.

If we rotate the connector output side in counter clockwise, we get numbers on output side as 1, 5, 2, 6, 3, 7, and 4.

89. **Answer:** Consider all the couples are on one bank, say Bank 1. Now we will explain the forward and return trips. Also we will indicate who the people on each bank are during and after the trip. The diagrammatic display of the situation as per the movement is given below:

'A, B, C, D, and E' indicate five men and 'a, b, c, d, and e' represent their respective wives. Woman 'a' knows operating the boat.

Sl No	Status	Bank 1 Position	In Boat	Bank 2 Position
1	Start	A, B, C, D, E, a, b, c, d, e		
2	Boat goes from Bank 1 to Bank 2	A, B, C, D, E, d, e	a, b, c	
3	Boat reaches Bank 2	A, B, C, D, E, d, e		a, b, c

4	Boat goes from Bank 2 to Bank 1	A, B, C, D, E, d, e	a	b, c
5	Boat reaches Bank 1	A, B, C, D, E, a, d, e		b, c
6	Boat goes from Bank 1 to Bank 2	A, B, C, D, E, e	a, b	b, c
7	Boat reaches Bank 2	A, B, C, D, E, e		a, b, c, d
8	Boat goes from Bank 2 to Bank 1	A, B, C, D, E, e	a	b, c, d
9	Boat reaches Bank 1	A, B, C, D, E, a, e		b, c, d
10	Boat goes from Bank 1 to Bank 2	A, E, a, e	B, C, D	b, c, d
11	Boat reaches Bank 2	A, E, a, e		B, C, D, b, c, d
12	Boat goes from Bank 2 to Bank 1	A, E, a, e	D, d	B, C, b, c
13	Boat reaches Bank 1	A, D, E, a, d, e		B, C, b, c
14	Boat goes from Bank 1 to Bank 2	D, E, d, e	A, a	B, C, b, c
15	Boat reaches Bank 2	D, E, d, e		A, B, C, a, b, c
16	Boat goes from Bank 2 to Bank 1	D, E, d, e	C, c	A, B, a, b
17	Boat reaches Bank 1	C, D, E, c, d, e		A, B, a, b
18	Boat goes from Bank 1 to Bank 2	c, d, e	C, D, E	A, B, a, b
19	Boat reaches Bank 2	c, d, e		A, B, C, D, E, a, b
20	Boat goes from Bank 2 to Bank 1	c, d, e	a	A, B, C, D, E, b

To derive full benefit, do not refer to the answer unless you make enough efforts to solve the puzzle.

21	Boat reaches Bank 1	a, c, d, e			A, B, C, D, E, b
22	Boat goes from Bank 1 to Bank 2	e		a, c, d	A, B, C, D, E, b
23	Boat reaches Bank 2	e			A, B, C, D, E, a, b, c, d
24	Boat goes from Bank 2 to Bank 1	e		a	A, B, C, D, E, b, c, d
25	Boat reaches Bank 1	a, e			A, B, C, D, E, b, c, d
26	Boat goes from Bank 1 to Bank 2			a, e	A, B, C, D, E, b, c, d
27	Boat reaches Bank 2				A, B, C, D, E, a, b, c, d, e

90. Answer: Pick one of the men and ask, "If I were to ask you whether the left fork leads to the town, and you chose to answer that question with the same way you answer this question, would you then answer 'yes'?"

Logic for the Solution: Note that Truth of a truth is truth and lie of a lie is also truth. (Positive of positive is positive and negative of negative is positive). We use this by embedding the question to answer twice of the same question. With this all the three men will give true answer. The person always telling truth will say "yes" if the left fork leads to the town (yes of yes is yes) and "no" otherwise. The liar will answer the same, since he will lie about where the left fork leads, and he will lie about lying (no of no is yes). The third man may either lie or tell the truth about this one question, but either way he is behaving like either the person telling the truth or the liar and thus must correctly report the road to your destination.

91. Answer: Five accounts were opened in SBI. Two accounts were opened in other than SBI.

Logic for the Solution: Three accounts, one by each viz. Poorwa, Sourabh and Neha were opened individually. Three were joint accounts by each pair i.e. Poorwa-Sourabh, Poorwa-Neha, and Sourabh-Neha. One was a joint account by all three. So there were seven accounts in total. We can see that each person had total of four accounts. Neha's four accounts were in SBI. Hence, all of the accounts of Neha were in SBI. These four accounts are: the one that Neha has individual, the one that Neha has jointly with Poorwa, the one that Neha has jointly with Sourabh and the one all three have together. This accounts for both of the SBI accounts Poorwa has, and two of the three SBI accounts Sourabh has. The third SBI account Sourabh has could not have been the one Poorwa and Sourabh have jointly, because Poorwa only has two SBI accounts. So the third SBI account Sourabh has must be the one that is individual. So five bank accounts were in SBI (the one Sourabh has, the one Neha has, the one Poorwa and Neha have jointly, the one Sourabh and Neha have jointly, and the one all three have jointly). The remaining two bank accounts are other than SBI (the one Poorwa has and the one Poorwa and Sourabh have jointly).

92. Answer: Order after first shuffle is: 9, A, 4, Q, J, 7, 3, 2, 10, 5, K, 8, 6

Logic for the Solution: The problem is solved by assuming positions for the first card in initial order i.e. ace, after the first shuffle. Then find the shuffle rule. Then position other cards as per the rule based on those assumptions, until one such assumption does not produce a conflict. Consider:

Initial Order	A	2	3	4	5	6	7	8	9	10	J	Q	K
First Shuffle Order		A											
Second Shuffle Order	10	9	Q	8	K	3	4	A	5	J	6	2	7

We will first assume the ace was in the second slot after the first shuffle. So the shuffling algorithm would always place the card in the first slot into the second slot. Therefore, the 9 must have been the first card after the first shuffle, or it couldn't have ended up as the second card after the second shuffle. So after the first shuffle position must be as follows.

Initial Order	A	2	3	4	5	6	7	8	9	10	J	Q	K
First Shuffle Order	9	A											
Second Shuffle Order	10	9	Q	8	K	3	4	A	5	J	6	2	7

Now that we know that the 9 must have been the first card after the first shuffle, we know that the shuffling algorithm takes the card in the ninth slot and puts it into the first slot. So after the first shuffle, the 10 must have been in the ninth slot, or the 10 would never have ended up as the first card after the second shuffle. So after the first shuffle position must be as follows.

Initial Order	A	2	3	4	5	6	7	8	9	10	J	Q	K
First Shuffle Order	9	A							10				
Second Shuffle Order	10	9	Q	8	K	3	4	A	5	J	6	2	7

We follow this logic pattern until our knowledge of the order of the cards after the first shuffle is complete. Now that we know that the 10 must have been the ninth card after the first shuffle. We know that the shuffling algorithm takes the card in the tenth slot and puts it into the ninth slot. So after the first shuffle, the 5 must have been in the tenth slot, or the 5 would never have ended up as the ninth card after the second shuffle. So after the first shuffle position must be as follows.

Initial Order	A	2	3	4	5	6	7	8	9	10	J	Q	K
First Shuffle Order	9	A							10	5			
Second Shuffle Order	10	9	Q	8	K	3	4	A	5	J	6	2	7

To derive full benefit, do not refer to the answer unless you make enough efforts to solve the puzzle.

Now we know that the shuffling algorithm takes the card in the fifth slot and puts it into the tenth slot. So after the first shuffle, the J must have been in the fifth slot, or the J would never have ended up as the tenth card after the second shuffle. So after the first shuffle position must be as follows.

Initial Order	A	2	3	4	5	6	7	8	9	10	J	Q	K
First Shuffle Order	9	A			J					10	5		
Second Shuffle Order	10	9	Q	8	K	3	4	A	5	J	6	2	7

Now we know that the shuffling algorithm takes the card in the eleventh slot and puts it into the fifth slot. So after the first shuffle, K must have been in the eleventh slot, or the K would never have ended up as the fifth card after the second shuffle. So after the first shuffle position must be as follows.

Initial Order	A	2	3	4	5	6	7	8	9	10	J	Q	K
First Shuffle Order	9	A			J					10	5	K	
Second Shuffle Order	10	9	Q	8	K	3	4	A	5	J	6	2	7

Now we know that the shuffling algorithm takes the card in the thirteenth slot and puts it into the eleventh slot. So after the first shuffle, 6 must have been in the thirteenth slot, or the 6 would never have ended up as the eleventh card after the second shuffle. So after the first shuffle position must be as follows.

Initial Order	A	2	3	4	5	6	7	8	9	10	J	Q	K
First Shuffle Order	9	A			J					10	5	K	6
Second Shuffle Order	10	9	Q	8	K	3	4	A	5	J	6	2	7

Now we know that the shuffling algorithm takes the card in the sixth slot and puts it into the thirteenth slot. So after the

To derive full benefit, do not refer to the answer unless you make enough efforts to solve the puzzle.

first shuffle, 7 must have been in the sixth slot, or the 7 would never have ended up as the eleventh card after the second shuffle. So after the first shuffle position must be as follows.

Initial Order	A	2	3	4	5	6	7	8	9	10	J	Q	K
First Shuffle Order	9	A			J	7			10	5	K		6
Second Shuffle Order	10	9	Q	8	K	3	4	A	5	J	6	2	7

Now we know that the shuffling algorithm takes the card in the seventh slot and puts it into the sixth slot. So after the first shuffle, 3 must have been in the seventh slot, or the 3 would never have ended up as the sixth card after the second shuffle. So after the first shuffle position must be as follows.

Initial Order	A	2	3	4	5	6	7	8	9	10	J	Q	K
First Shuffle Order	9	A			J	7	3		10	5	K		6
Second Shuffle Order	10	9	Q	8	K	3	4	A	5	J	6	2	7

Now we know that the shuffling algorithm takes the card in the third slot and puts it into the seventh slot. So after the first shuffle, 4 must have been in the third slot, or the 4 would never have ended up as the seventh card after the second shuffle. So after the first shuffle position must be as follows.

Initial Order	A	2	3	4	5	6	7	8	9	10	J	Q	K
First Shuffle Order	9	A	4		J	7	3		10	5	K		6
Second Shuffle Order	10	9	Q	8	K	3	4	A	5	J	6	2	7

Now we know that the shuffling algorithm takes the card in the fourth slot and puts it into the third slot. So after the first shuffle, Q must have been in the fourth slot, or the Q would never have ended up as the third card after the second shuffle. So after the first shuffle position must be as follows.

To derive full benefit, do not refer to the answer unless you make enough efforts to solve the puzzle.

Initial Order	A	2	3	4	5	6	7	8	9	10	J	Q	K
First Shuffle Order	9	A	4	Q	J	7	3		10	5	K		6
Second Shuffle Order	10	9	Q	8	K	3	4	A	5	J	6	2	7

Now we know that the shuffling algorithm takes the card in the twelfth slot and puts it into the fourth slot. So after the first shuffle, 8 must have been in the twelfth slot, or the 8 would never have ended up as the fourth card after the second shuffle. So after the first shuffle position must be as follows.

Initial Order	A	2	3	4	5	6	7	8	9	10	J	Q	K
First Shuffle Order	9	A	4	Q	J	7	3		10	5	K	8	6
Second Shuffle Order	10	9	Q	8	K	3	4	A	5	J	6	2	7

Finally we fill 2 in the eighth place after first shuffle.

It turns out that this is the correct answer. If we assume the ace to be in any other position other than the second, then we will eventually encounter a contradiction, where two cards must go into the same slot.

So the final ordering is: **9, A, 4, Q, J, 7, 3, 2, 10, 5, K, 8, 6.**

93. **Answer:** A can see B and C. If A sees two black hats or two white hats, then he would be able to tell the color of his hat as he knows two hats are black and two white. But if, he sees one white and one black hat, he would not be sure of colour of his hat. So he would keep quiet. Some time passes, and B would realizes that 1 is not sure what color hat he's wearing. The only way A wouldn't be sure is if B and C are wearing differently colored hats. Now B, who sees what color hat C is wearing, can correctly tell colour of his hat as the opposite colour of the hat that C is wearing.

Logic for Solution: Not communicating is also a method of communication!!

94. Answer: The difference of height would be one and half feet. The mark on the hand would be 3 feet above the ground and nail mark on the tree would be one and half feet from the ground. Thus the mark on the body would be one and half feet above the mark on the tree.

Logic for the Solution: Tree grows from above. Hence the nail mark would not move. Whereas the human body grows proportionately. Thus Nail would remain at the same height and tattoo will move to the height twice to its original position.

95. Answer: It is not possible.

Logic for Solution: While drawing a circuit every time we move out from a vertex and again enter the vertex. Thus every time we visit a vertex we remove two edges is we are not allowed to use same path again. Hence to have a close loop without tracing or retracting the same path, the edges joining at the vertex must be even, one for entering and one for leaving. This is also called as 'Euler Circuit' in graph theory. In this problem all vertices have odd number of edges emanating from it (five each). Hence 'Euler Circuit' cannot be drawn. Hence it is not possible to trace the figure without lifting your pen or tracing a line more than once.

Note: It is possible to draw such a circuit if vertices have even number of edges. For example,

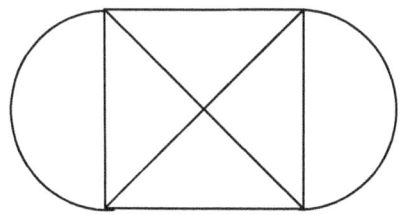

96. Answer: 125 boxes have been used.

Logic for Solution: By putting 10 boxes in one box, the total number of empty boxes on the table is increases by 10 - 1 = 9. This is because the 10 boxes put inside other box are empty but the box in which these are put becomes filled thus reducing the number of empty boxes on the table by one. Let x be the number of times sourabh has put 10 boxes in an empty after putting 15 empty boxes on the table. Hence we can write an equation for number of empty boxes as,

$15 + 9x = 114$.

It follows that x=11. Now after putting 15 empty boxes on the table every time Sourabh filled a box, he added 10 boxes in the total. Hence total number of boxes used by Sourabh is,

$15 + 11 \times 10 = 125$.

97. Answer: The captain recommends that front two members to be put the same colour hats. Remaining two hats could be put on to other two in any order.

Logic for the Solution: There are four hats in three colours; red, white, and blue. Means two hats must be of the same colour and other two in remaining different colours. Suppose there are two blue hats. (This considered arbitrarily. Same logic is applicable to any colours).

Now as per the captain's recommendation the two team members standing in front must be put on blue hats. Let's suppose the third member from front was put on red hat, and the fourth member (member in the rear) was put there maining white hat. The member standing in rearwould be the first to answer. Since he sees two blue hatsand one red hat worn by the members in front of him, he would be certain that his hat is white. On the other hand if he had seen front two members wearing blue hats and third member wearing white hat, obviously the rear member would know that he is wearing the red hat. So he would answer correctly. Now the third member from the front could tell the colour of his hat correctly since he has heard the answer of rear member and could see front two members wearing blue hats. So if the rear member had announced colour of his hat as white, the third member would tell colour of his hat as red. On the other hand if the rear member had told his hat colour as red, the third member would tell colour of his hat as white. Now since the rear two members have told colours of their hats confidently, the front two members know that both of them are wearing same colour blue hats. Because, if it was not so, both the rear members would not have been able to say colours of their correctly and confidently. Same logic extends irrespective of colour of the two identical hats.

Now let us see what happens if two blue colour hats (we have selected blue colour arbitrarily) are not put on to front two members. Suppose one of the blue colour hats is put on to rear member. In that case the rear member would see three members in front of him wearing three different colour hats. In that case he would not be able to tell the color of his own hat, since the duplicate color could be any of them. Therefore, he must see two hats of the same color (blue) and one hat of a second color. Only then he can state conclusively the colour of his hat; namely the third color.

Now let us see if the hat with duplicate colour is put on to the third member from the front. In this case rear person can tell colour of his hat. However, the third from the front would have problem. He knows the colour of the hat worn by rear person as he has announced it correctly. But he would see hats of both remaining colours worn by the members in the front. In that case he would not be able to tell the color of his own hat, since the duplicate color could be any of them. Therefore, he must see two hats of the same color (blue) in front and hear correct answer from the rear member. Only then he can state conclusively the colour of his hat; namely the third color.

This logic uses negation. You eliminate the possibilities based on your observations and pick the last left option. Further you use information given by the members behind you and also

To derive full benefit, do not refer to the answer unless you make enough efforts to solve the puzzle.

the fact that they have given the answers indicates to you what they would have seen to be so confident.

98. Answer: Build three cages and put three birds in each. (Or put any combination like 1, 3, and 5). Then build a fourth cage around the other three cages. So the outer cage would have 9 birds.

Logic for Solution: Cage in side cage does not add up the odd number of birds. Once you understand this method you can have many different ways. For example, keep all 9 birds in one cage and then build other cages one around other in a sequences.

99. Answer: Suppose the first man is A, the second man B, and the third man C. There are six cases. These are:

Case	A	B	C
I	Speaks Truth	Liar	Random
II	Speaks Truth	Random	Liar
III	Liar	Speaks Truth	Random
IV	Liar	Random	Speaks Truth
V	Random	Speaks Truth	Liar
VI	Random	Liar	Speaks Truth

Now we ask question in the order given below to determine which possibility mentioned above is correct:

Ask A, "Is B more likely to tell the truth than C?"

a) If he says "Yes", then cases I and III can be ruled out. Then ask C, "Are you the random man?"
   i) If he says "No", cases II and V could be ruled out. Then ask C "Is A liar?" If he says "Yes", the case IV is the answer. If he says "No", the case VI is the answer.
   ii) If he says "Yes", then cases IV and VI can be eliminated. So we have only cases II and V. Then ask C, "Is A always tells the truth?" If he says "Yes", case V is the answer. If he says "No", case II is the answer.

To derive full benefit, do not refer to the answer unless you make enough efforts to solve the puzzle.

b) If he says "No", Then II and IV cases can be ruled out. Then ask B, "Are you the random man?"

   i) If he says "Yes", cases III and V could be ruled out. Then ask B "Is A always tell the truth? If he answers "Yes" the answer is case VI. If he says "No" the case I is the answer.

   ii) If he says "No", cases I and VI could be ruled out. Then ask B "Is A liar?" If the reply is "Yes" case III is the answer. If the reply is "No" then case V is the answer.

Thus asking only three questions in sequence depending on the answers to the previous questions we can with certainty determine the identities of the three men.

Logic for the Solution: We have asked first question to A relating B and C such that we eliminate two cases either when B speaks Random in both or C speaks Random in both. Thus after first question either B or C does not have cases of Random. Now for second question select B or C for asking question that does not have choice of Random. Now it is simple to find logic to reduce options from 4 to 2 and then 2 to 1 with one question each.

100. **Answer:** You light one fuse at both ends and, at the same time, light the second fuse at one end. When the first fuse has completely burnt, you know that a half an hour has elapsed. So now you know that the second fuse has exactly half an hour left to go. At this time, you light the second fuse from the other end. This will cause it to burn out in another 15 minutes. At that point, exactly 45 minutes would have elapsed. Now you confidently fire two flair shots. Helicopter will locate you and rescue your team.

Logic for Solution: Rate of burning can be doubled or time of burning could be halved by burning a fuse wire from both the ends.

101. **Answer:** Yes. No matter how he varies his travel speed within the two trips, there must indeed be such a point somewhere along the path.

Logic for the Solution: An easy way to visualize this is to imagine, instead of one man making one trip and then making the return trip, two men making the trip at the same time. One man leaves the home at 1pm and heads toward the office. The other leaves the office at 1pm and heads toward the home. Regardless of their speed over the course of the journey, they must pass each other on their respective journeys at some point. Thus they must be at the same place at the same time. (Well this point may not be the midpoint, but they would be at same point at same time. The point itself may change from day to day. But it would exist on every day).

102. **Answer:** It is not possible.

Logic for the Solution: Consider all land masses as vertices A, B, C and D. Consider the bridges as edges joining the vertices. Thus we get an undirected graph. It would look like,

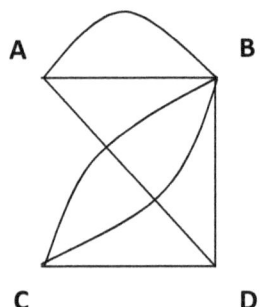

While drawing a circuit every time we move out from a vertex and again enter the vertex. Thus every time we visit a vertex we remove two edges is we are not allowed to use same path again. Hence to have a close loop without tracing or retracting the same path, the edges joining at the vertex must be even, one for entering and one for leaving. This is also called as 'Euler Circuit' in graph theory. Since in this problem vertices have odd number of edges emanating from it, Euler Circuit cannot be drawn. Hence it is not possible to start at some location in the town, travel across all bridges without crossing any bridge twice, and return to the starting point.

103. Answer:

	7				7	
4	1	3		3	1	4
6	8	5		5	8	6
	2				2	

Logic for the Solution: Number 1 and 8 have only one adjacent number between numbers 1 to 8. Hence we put these in two middle squares. Obviously numbers 2 and 7 have only one location each that are not adjacent to numbers 1 and 8 that are already placed. Now we can put numbers 3 and 4. There are two ways to avoid touching number 3 to 1. We can select any. There are two ways for number 4 without touching 3. We can select only opposite 3 since after placing 4 the remaining box next to it cannot accommodate 5 and also that box can accommodate 6 if it is not near 7. Now place number 5 next to 3 and 6 next to 4. Both these numbers are away from 7.

104. **Answer:** Both would confess and get 6 months punishment each.

Logic of the Solution: Although there is more efficient solution that both of then 'don't confess' and get 1 month punishment each. However, they are not likely to select it. Because any one selects this option and the other confesses, the prisoner not confessing would get 9 month punishment. Whereas the prisoner confessing will go free. Since none of them are sure of other's decision, both will confess. This solution is called as Pareto inefficient stable solution. (This is a classic problem of game theory and known as Prisoner's Dilemma.

105. **Answer:** Four colours.

Logic of the Solution: The solution was guessed quote long. But there is no analytical proof for this answer. Mathematicians were working on it for more than 200 years. It was finally proved using computers in 1976. This is known as four colour theorem. It states that the chromatic number of a planer graph is no greater than four. (Try for analytical proof. Never know you may be successful). Incidentally this led to Graph Colouring theory. This can be effectively used for optimizing examination schedule so that examination can be conducted in minimum number of days without any student getting two examinations at the same time! (I don't know if they use it in any university!!)

106. **Answer:** Tree A had 5 birds and tree B had 7 birds.

Logic of the Solution: We could solve it by algebraic method. Let X and Y are the number of birds on trees A and B respectively. Now we can write two equations for two conditions as $2(X - 1) = Y + 1$ and $X + 1 = Y - 1$. Now by solving these simultaneous equations for X and Y we get $X = 5$ and $Y = 7$.

If we want to find the answer logically without using algebraic calculations (solving simultaneous equations), we work as follows. One bird from the tree B when flies to tree A makes number of birds equal. Hence there is a difference of two birds between trees A and B. Also when one bird from the tree A flies to the tree B, it makes number of birds on the tree B twice as that of number of birds on the tree A. Thus after one bird flying to tree B the number of birds on the tree B must be even. Therefore before one bird flies from the tree A to B, the number of birds on the tree B must be odd. Hence from these two statement we need to check the possible combinations of the birds on the trees A and B are (1, 3), (3, 5), (5, 7), (7, 9) etc. We can easily rule out first two and fourth onwards are not possible to meet the conditions. Thus answer is the combination (5, 7).

107. Answer: Yes. a-b-d-g-h-j-i-h-k-g-j-d-c-b-e-i-f-e-a

Logic of the Solution: This has all vertices with even edges. Hence Euler circuit is possible. However, we should be careful not to leave any outer nodes hanging without any approaching edge. For this we need to obtain a sub graph deleting these edges that make the vertices isolated. Then trace the sub graph splicing it at appropriate places to including the isolated vertices.

108. Answer: 255

Logic of the Solution: We can develop a recurrence relation for the problem and then solve it. Let there be 'n' discs. Let an is the number of steps required to move the 'n' discs with following the rules. So for 'n – 1' discs number of steps are an-1 steps. Now from 'n' discs we move 'n-1' discs in an-1 steps from first to third peg. Then move last disc from first peg to second peg in one move. Finally we move 'n-1' discs in an-1 steps from third peg to second peg. Hence,

$a_n = 2 \times X_{an-1} + 1$

So $a_8 = 2 \times Xa_7 + 1$, $a_7 = 2 \times Xa_6 + 1$ etc. With $a_1 = 1$ we can solve the problem easily.

[This is a recurrence relation. We can find solution to this as $a_n = 2^n - 1$. For proof you can refer my book 'Probability and Combinatorics' if you are so interested. This is a popular puzzle in century invented by the French mathematician Edourd Lucas known as 'The Tower of Hanoi'. A myth was created to market the puzzle. It says "At the tower in Hanoi, a monk is transferring 64 gold discs from one peg to another in similar fashion as the puzzle. Each disc transfer takes one second. When the monk will finish the work, the world would end"! However we need not worry because from the explicit formula that we will prove later, minimum number of moves required for completing the transfer 64 discs are,

$2^n - 1 = 2^{64} - 1$ -18,446, 744,073,709,551,615.

Thus the time taken is more than 500 billion years!! So world should survive a while longer than it already has!!! And in any case we won't be there to witness this end of world!!!!]

109. Answer: Join centers of the rectangular paper and rectangular removed portion. This can be easily done by joining diagonals. (For the cut portion keep the paper on other paper and join the corners of cut portion to get its center). Extend this line on both sides. Cut the paper on this line.

Logic of the Solution: Any line passing through the center of a rectangle always splits the rectangular area in half. So a line through the center of the rectangular paper will split the rectangular paper in to half. Similarly line passing through the center of the rectangular cut will split the removed area in to half. So the line passing through the center of rectangular paper and also rectangular cut will split the paper in two pieces whose uncut paper areas are equal as well areas of removed cut rectangle are also equal. Hence both pieces would have equal areas. This is equal to (Area of paper − Area of cut)/2. This is shown below. Cutting line is A − B.

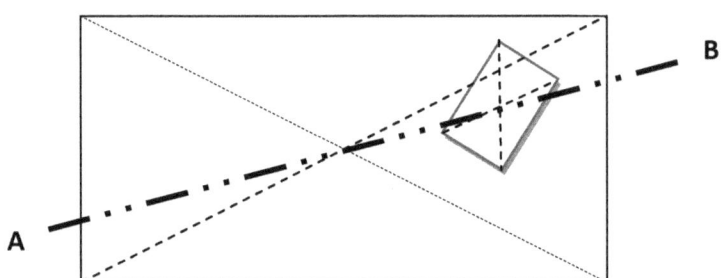

110. Answer: Tree A had 3 birds and tree B had 5 birds.

Logic of the Solution: We could solve it by algebraic method. Let X and Y are the number of birds on trees A and B respectively. Now we can write two equations for two conditions as $3(X - 1) = Y + 1$ and $X + 1 = Y - 1$. Now by solving these simultaneous equations for X and Y we get $X = 3$ and $Y = 5$.

If we want to find the answer logically without using algebraic calculations (solving simultaneous equations), we work as follows. One bird from the tree B when flies to tree A makes number of birds equal. Hence there is a difference of two birds between trees A and B. Also when one bird from the tree A flies to the tree B, it makes number of birds on the tree B thrice as the number of birds on the tree A. Thus before one bird flies to the tree B, the number of birds on the tree B must be a number one less than multiple of three like 2, 5, 8, 11 etc. Hence from these two statement we need to check the possible combinations of the birds on the trees A and B are (3, 5), (6, 8), (9, 11) etc. We can easily find the right combination as (3, 5).

111. **Answer:** The steps and position of values in different location is given below.

Steps	Values in the Locations		
	A	B	C
Starts	X	Y	Z
C = A → C	X	Y	X
A = A − C	0	Y	X
C = B → C	0	Y	Y
A = A − C	−Y	Y	Y
C = A → C	−Y	Y	−Y
A = A − C	0	Y	−Y
A = A − C	Y	Y	−Y

Now we have value Y in location A.

112. **Answer:** $\frac{3n}{2} - 2$ For example in case of collection of 100 randomly selected numbers minimum number of steps to find highest and lowest numbers would require 148 comparisons.

Logic for the Solution: Take two numbers at a time. Compare them and put smaller number in one array (or bin) and larger number in second array (or bin). Continue the process in similar manner collecting smaller among a pair in first array and larger among the pair in second array. For 'n' numbers we have to compare $\frac{n}{2}$ pairs. Thus there are $\frac{n}{2}$ comparisons. Obviously the lowest number is in the first array and highest number is in second array. Both arrays are of have $\frac{n}{2}$ numbers each. For finding out lowest number in first array we need $\frac{n}{2}$ -1 comparisons and for finding out highest number from the second array we need $\frac{n}{2}$ -1 comparisons. Thus total number of comparisons is $\frac{n}{2} + \frac{n}{2} - 1 + \frac{n}{2} - 1 = \frac{3n}{2} - 2$. For 100 numbers the answer is 148.

Note 1: If we follow most efficient sorting method viz. heap sort, number of comparison operations are × ln (n) . For 100 numbers heap sort takes 460 compare operations. Of course it completely sorts the array where as we only want smallest and largest numbers.

Note 2: Another method is to first find smallest number with n-1 comparisons and then after removing that number find the highest number with n-2 comparisons. Thus total comparisons are 2n-3. For 100 numbers this process would require 197 comparisons.

113. **Answer:** Moved matchsticks are shown by dotted lines.

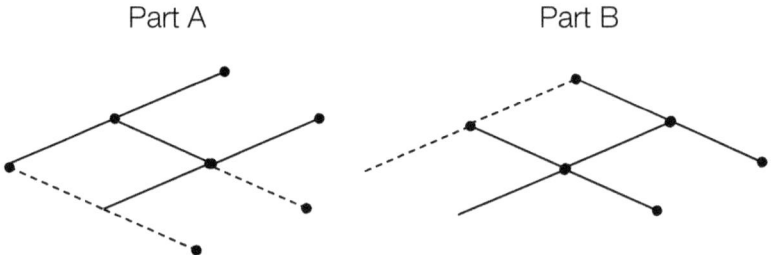

Part A   Part B

Logic of the Solution: First mark those lines which could also form the part of the fish in other direction without shifting them. This is shown below for both parts. Other unmarked matchsticks are shown as dotted lines.

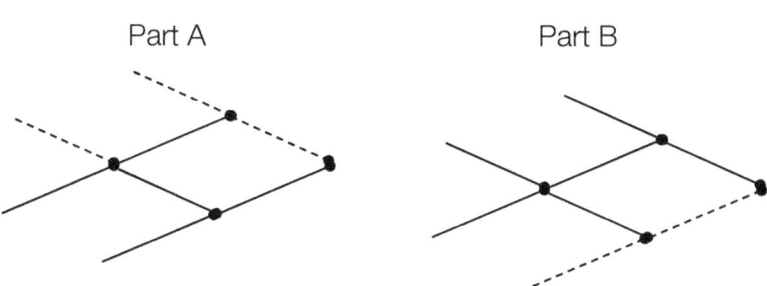

Part A   Part B

Now we can easily decide where to move these dotted matchsticks to get the fish with changed direction as desired.

114. **Answer:** Moved matchsticks are shown by dotted lines.

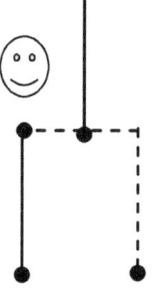

115. **Answer:** First the front horse from left convoy moves one length forward in available gap. This would change the position as,

Then front horse from right jumps over the first horse from left and the second horse from the right moves one place in front taking the place of the first horse that has jumped. The situation would be,

Then front horse from left jumps over the second horse from the right, second horse from left jumps over the first horse from the right and the third horse from the left moves one place in front taking the place of the second horse that has jumped. The situation would be,

To derive full benefit, do not refer to the answer unless you make enough efforts to solve the puzzle.

Then the front horse from right jumps over the third horse on left, then fourth horse on left and moves on. After that the second horse on the right jumps over the second horse on left, then third and then fourth on the left and then moves on. After that the third horse on the right jumps over the first horse on left, then second, third and then fourth on the left and then moves on. Then fourth horse on right moves one place forward. After that the fourth horse on the right jumps over the first horse on left, then second, third and then fourth on the left and then moves on. Now the horses on the left could walk straight one by one and clear the bridge.

116.   Answer: Deepak and Poorwa both do not like Keshar-Pista and Sandhya's favorite flavour is either Butter scotch or Mango. Hence Sourabh's must have picked Keshar-Pista. Sandhya's flavour should be Mango. The person who likes Chocolate is a girl. As it is not that of Sandhya's, so Poorwa's flavour must be Chocolate. Deepak's flavour cannot be Keshar-Pista and Chocolate, it might be Mango or Butter scotch. As Sandhya's flavour is Mango, so Deepak's flavour will be Butter scotch.

Logic of the Solution: Usually initially pick up negative statements to eliminate some of the possibilities. With this we can match few initial pairs. Then remaining

117.   Answer: Gold is in the first box.

Logic of the Solution: Only one message is true. If that true message is on the first box. Then gold is in second or third box. In both cases either the messages on the second or third box would be true. Hence the gold must be in the first box.

Let us test it. If the message on the first box is lie, the message on the second box is true and message on the third box is lie. Hence it satisfies the condition. Check other possibilities. If the gold is in second box, the statements on the first and third boxes would be true and hence it is contradictory to the condition. If the gold is in third box, the statements on the first and second boxes would be true and hence it is contradictory to the condition.

118. Answer: These numbers are one squared, two squared, three squared, four squared, and so on up to 10 squared. So, ten lights would be 'ON'.

Logic of the Solution: The only lights with numbers as perfect squares (1, 4, 9, 16, etc) would remain 'ON'. Because they are the only numbers divisible by an odd number of whole numbers; every factor other than the number's square root is paired up with another. Thus, these switch will be 'changed' an odd number of times, (including first operation) which means they will be left 'ON'. All the other numbers are divisible by an even number of factors and will consequently end up 'OFF'. Note if number A has 'a' as a factor, it implies that $A = a \times b$ where a and b are integers. Thus, for every factor 'a' there is another corresponding factor 'b'. Also note that $A = 1 \times A$. Thus 1 pairs with A. If the number is a prime, it has only two factors viz. 1 and the number itself. Only in case of the perfect square $A = a \times a$, so the divisor 'a' is not paired with another number. So the number of lights 'ON' is the number of perfect squares less than or equal to 100.

119. Answer: 45

Logic of the Solution: There are many logics for the solution. Here are few.

The given table with labels is shown below.

	A	b	c	d	e
1	2	3	4	15	12
2	3	4	5	28	20
3	4	5	6	X	30
4	5	6	7	66	42
5	6	7	8	91	56

1. We can see the rule: $d = (a + b) \times b$
   This is true for rows 1, 2, 4 and 5.
   Hence for the row 3, $X = d_3 = (4 + 5) \times 5 = 45$

To derive full benefit, do not refer to the answer unless you make enough efforts to solve the puzzle.

2. We can see the rule: $d = e + b \times i$ Where i = row number
   This is true for rows 1, 2, 4 and 5.
   Hence for the row 3 (i.e. $i = 3$), $X = d_3 = 30 + 5 \times (3) = 45$
3. We can see the rule: $d_{i+1} - d_i = 13 + 4 \times (i - 1)$
   where i = row number.
   This is true for rows 2 and 5 ($i = 1$ and $i = 4$). Thus for row 3 ($i = 2$),
   $d_3 - d_2 = 13 + 4 \times (2 - 1) = 17$
   $X = d_3 = d_2 + 21 = 28 + 17 = 45$
   Also for row 4 ($i = 3$),
   $d_4 - d_3 = 13 + 4 \times (3 - 1) = 21$
   $X = d_3 = d_4 - 21 = 66 - 21 = 45$
   Hence we get the answer.
4. We can see the rule: $d = b \times (c + i)$ Where i = row number
   This is true for rows 1, 2, 4 and 5.
   Hence for the row 3 (i.e. $i = 3$), $X = d_3 = 5 \times (6 + 3) = 45$

120. **Answer: One Rupee did not come from anywhere. We had Rs 50 and we spend Rs 50**

Logic for Solution: This is just a trick to confuse us. If you check carefully one side is of spending. If you have Rs 50 and finally the balance is zero obviously the total of money spent is Rs 50. There is no specific relationship between the total of money spend and total of balance. So comparing them with each other has no meaning. Just to prove the argument I will show few examples.

	Example 1		Example 2	
	Money Spend Rs	Balance Rs	Money Spend Rs	Balance Rs
	1	49	50	0
	1	48		
	1	47		
	47	0		
Total	50	144	50	0

To derive full benefit, do not refer to the answer unless you make enough efforts to solve the puzzle.

Thus the total of the balance can be anything from 0 (if Rs 50 spent at one time) to 1225 (if we consider Rs 1 spend every time for 50 times. Note this is Sum of 1+2+3+.....+49= (49x50)/2 i.e. being sum of first 'n' numbers which is (n) x(n+1)/2

Algebraic way to explain is we started with say Rs 'P' spend is say Rs 'a, b, c' in three steps, the balance would be 'P – a', 'P – a –b', 'P – a – b – c'. So the Total of the Money Spend is 'a + b + c'. This must be P. Thus, a + b + c = P. On the other hand Total of Balance is '3P – 3a – 2b – c'. Substituting value of P the Total of Balance is 'b+2c'. This cannot be equal to P in general as numbers 'a, b, and c' are chosen arbitrarily. Obviously total of money spend and total of balance cannot be equal. Only they will be equal when P = b + 2C. For example b = 10 and c = 20 hence a = 20. Check yourself. There are many combinations like this. For example a 15, b = 20 and c = 15. Find some more. Have you noted that in all such combinations a = c

121.   **Answer: Family is,**

A- Grandfather H-Grandmother D-Son C-Daughter in law E-Daughter G-Son in Law B-Grand Son (Son's Son) F-Grand Daughter (Daughter's Daughter)

Sitting clock wise A-C-G-H-D-F- B-E

Logic of the Solution: First we fix the relationship of various persons and also identify them as male and female. This will help us in finding their relative position on a table. First we consider the two facts that there are eight members, of whom three are married couples, there is no widower / widow and no two male members are sitting adjacent to each other. Thus there can only be three or four male members. Let us find them. A is a grandfather, a male member. B is a nephew, a male member. D is a son, a male member. G is a father a male member. Thus A, B, D and G are male members. Hence C, E, F and G must be female members. Statements 1 and 4 implies G is son in law or son of A. Statement 2 indicates E is either a daughter or daughter in law of A. As per statement 2, B has aunt / uncle and also father in the gathering, indicates that he belongs to third generation. Thus we identify A from first generation, B and F are from third generation, and others must be from first and second generation because B and F are cousins and cannot be a couple. Statement 3 indicates H is from first generation as D is a son of H. Thus H is a grandmother. As per statement G is a father of F, hence D must be a father of B. Now from the second statement E is a daughter of A and H, wife of G and mother of F. Finally C is a wife of D.

Now let us consider sitting arrangement. Male members must sit alternately to satisfy sentence 7. From the first statement we can start from one position and right B-X-A. (X means we still do not know). From second statement the position is D-X-B-A. Therefore we can find the position of males as clockwise as A-X-G-X-D-X-B-X. (Since it a circle we can start from anyone, we started from A, respect for grandfather!), Statement 3 fixes position of E and we get clockwise positions as A-X-G-X-D-X-B-E. Statement 5 fixes position of C as she cannot be next to D. Hence we get clock wise positions as A-C-G-X-D-X-B-E. Statement 5 also prohibits F to sit opposite to E and hence the position is Clockwise A-C-G-X-D-F-B-E. Now the last person left is grandmother H, who can occupy the empty seat. Thus the answer is Sitting clock wise A-C-G-H-D-F-B-E.

122.   Answer: Rs 1000

Logic of the Solution:

(a) Shop keeper has a counterfeit note of Rs 1000. This obviously his loss as he is keeping counterfeit note as if it was good note. So before he realized this there was no loss. But once he knows it and has to return the money to the next shop his loss is Rs 1000

(b) Another way to look at it is as follows. The counterfeit note has no value. What the shopkeeper has lost is Rs 800 he has returned to the lady plus the goods of Rs 200 he gave to the lady without getting money for the goods. So the total loss is Rs 1000

To derive full benefit, do not refer to the answer unless you make enough efforts to solve the puzzle.

123. Answer: 121

Logic of the Solution: The flea can end up at most 10 jumps to the right, left, up, or down. We can inductively show that the sum of coefficients of the lattice point that the flea is on has the same parity as the number of jumps that the flea has taken. Hence, the flea cannot end up at a lattice point that is an odd number of jumps away from the origin. Now from origin we take ten jumps. Thus the n = 11 (origin 0,0 to 10,0 or -10,0 or 0,10 or 0,-10 as extreme corner points of square lattice) The set of possible ending lattice points forms a diamond square shape in the plane. Number of lattice points with nth centered square is given by C4,11 = n2 + (n-1)2 out of these lattice points, n2 have even parity and (n-1)2 have odd parity. (This is because in our case we have even jumps. It would be odd parity if our jumps were odd). Thus the flea can reach with 10 jumps to 11x11=121 lattice points. (Flea cannot end on remaining lattice square points). It is easy to see that each of these lattice points can be reached through exactly 10 jumps. For example, take an even number of jumps to reach the point, the jump up and down till the total number of jumps is 10. So the number of possible ending lattice points is 121.

Note: If you find it difficult to understand draw picture for cases of 2 jumps and 4 jumps.

Mathematical Explanation:

The pictures below suggests a solution when the flea makes exactly 0, 1, 2 and 3 jumps instead of 10.

The nth centered square number is given by the formula

$$C_{4,n} = n^2 + (n - 1)^2.$$

In other words, a centered square number is the sum of two consecutive square numbers. The following pattern demonstrates this formula and shows

No of possible Lattice Ending Points N

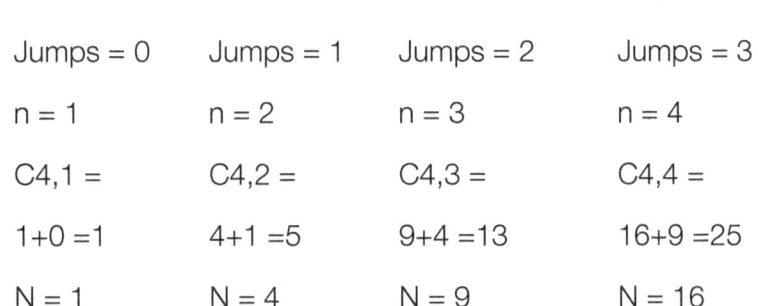

Jumps = 0	Jumps = 1	Jumps = 2	Jumps = 3
n = 1	n = 2	n = 3	n = 4
C4,1 =	C4,2 =	C4,3 =	C4,4 =
1+0 =1	4+1 =5	9+4 =13	16+9 =25
N = 1	N = 4	N = 9	N = 16

Hence for Jumps = 10 i.e. n = 11, C4, 11 = 121 + 100

Therefore, N = 121

124. **Answer: No one really had any effective debt before and after**

Logic of the Solution: This is simple. If you look carefully no one had any net liability. There was equal amount of debt and credit. So it is just neutralized on paper. Earlier also all were without net liability and now also. Consider you borrow from me Rs 1000 and then I also borrow Rs 1000 from you without you paying me as return of loan. That's what happens when we keep FD in bank and then take a loan against it. Only difference is we are fool and the bank is smart. It gives loan at higher interest rate and takes FD on lower to make money.

125. **Answer: What we just did was to subtract your year of birth from the present year. Obviously it will give your age. The 49 was just to confuse you. 49 through multiplication became 4900 and hence provided the place of two digits to your age.**

Note that this will not work if your age is above 99.

Logic of the Solution: Take a number X (here 49 which could be any two digit number). Multiply by 2 so it becomes 2X. Add 5 to make 2X + 5. Multiply by 50 to make 100X + 250. Now already the 49 has become 4900. The important trick is to make balance number 250 as current year (in this case 2014). So Add 1764 to make it 100X + 2014. Now if we subtract the birth year, 2014 – birth year will obviously give age.

Note: Depending on the current year you need to add a number. In 2014 it was 1764, in year 2015 it would be 1765 and so on so that adding it to 250 it makes current year.

126. **Answer: 80 Orange toffees, 1 Coffee bite and 19 Chocolate toffees**

Logic of the Solution: We have to do small algebra here. Let quantities each of orange toffees, coffee bite toffees and chocolate toffees be X, Y and Z respectively. We can write equations as,

$X+Y+Z=100$ \hspace{2cm} Total toffees

$\frac{1}{20}X+Y+5Z=100$ \hspace{2cm} Money spent

Subtracting the two equations,

$\frac{19}{20}X-5Z=0$

Or, $19X=80Z$

The only way we can get X as integer if Z is a multiple of 19. Obviously, any number like 38, 57 etc. are not feasible as the cost would be more than Rs 100. So only possibility is Z = 19 Hence, X = 80 and Y = 1

127. **Answer: 40 Squares**

Logic of the Solution: If you observe carefully and count all squares systematically, there are: one square of size 4x4, four square of size 3x3, nine square of size 2x2, eighteen square of size 1x1 and eight square of size (1/4)x(1/4). Thus the total number of squares is 40.

128. **Answer: July 16**

Logic of the Solution: If the birthday was May 19 or June 18, Nachiket would have known it just by knowing date without month. In the first sentence Poorwa after knowing the month is so confident that Nachiket does not know the birthday implies that the month that she knows must be July or August. Otherwise she won't have been confident that irrespective of knowing only the date, Nachiket does not know the birthday. Now knowing her confidence, Nachiket would rightly guess the month is not May or June. He knows the date. Now he is confident that he knows birthday means the date he knew that it cannot be 14, because he cannot decide between July 14 and August 14. Thus birthday could only be on August 15, August 17 or July 16. Now knowing confidence of Nachiket, Poorwa becomes certain about the birthday. It was not possible for her if the month told to her by Girish was August as there would have been two possibilities August 15 and August 17. Now since she is certain about the birthday in third statement implies that the month told to her by Girish must be July. Hence the birthday is July 16. Only this day satisfies all the three sentences.

129. **Answer:** The colour of his hat is White.

Logic for Solution: Since there are two black hats in five, there can be at the most two black hats out of three they are finally wearing. Let us indicate the hat colour white as 'W' and black as 'B'. So the possible orders of hats as the rear, middle and front person wearing would be WWW, BWW, WBW, WWB, and WBB. Now if the rear person see both the people in front of him are wearing black hats, he would have easily guessed his / her hat as white and said so to win the price. But the rear person had said "I don't know the colour of my hat". So WBB possibility is ruled out. So the possible combinations for the middle and front person are WW, BW or WB. Now if the middle person had seen that the front person is wearing a black hat. The only possible combination being WB, he would have guessed his / her hat as white. However, the middle person had said "I don't know the colour of my hat". This means combination WB is ruled out. Now from the remaining possible combinations the only possible colour for the front person is white. So he is confident and guesses the colour of his / her hat as white.

130. **Answer:** You give one of the friend a mango with basket. So his mango is in the basket.

131. **Answer:** The distribution is 98, 0, 1, 0, 1 in the order of seniority.

Logic for Solution: Here every person is to maximize his / her reward. Now let us see the reverse way. Let us name the persons in order of the seniority of their age as A, B, C, D and C. Now let us consider if in the process A, B and C are voted out and only D and E are left. Then D will distribute the gold coins as 100, 0 and vote in favour. Since he / she can get 50% of votes he / she keeps 100 coins and E gets nothing. Hence it is not in the interest of E to vote such that C is voted out when only three of them are remaining. Now let us consider what happens when only three persons C, D and E are remaining after A and B are voted out. Now C is the senior most and maximize his benefit, obviously he will distribute the coins as 99, 0, 1. Now since 1 is better than nothing, E would vote in favour and C will of course vote in favour. So C gets 99 coins E gets 1 coin and D gets nothing. Obviously D won't like this situation. Hence he / she will ensure that this situation won't arise. In other words D would not vote out B. Now go back to the situation when B was there. When B, C, D and E are there, B will distribute 98, 0, 1, 0. Now Dget 1 coin. If he / she votes against so as to vote out B, he / shewill get nothing in the next round. So D will vote in favour and of course B will vote in favour to get 50% votes to win the distribution. This is no good situation for C and E. So they won't like to reach this situation by voting out A. So they will ensure that A is not voted out. When all were in the game, A distributed as 98, 0, 1, 0, 1. This is a better situation for C and E than the next. Hence both will vote in favour. A would of course vote in favour. Thus the vote wins by more than 50%. Hence the final distribution is 98, 0, 1, 0, 1 for A, B, C, D and E respectively.

<small>To derive full benefit, do not refer to the answer unless you make enough efforts to solve the puzzle.</small>

LOGIRIDDLES

132. Answer: The distribution is 97, 0, 1, 0, 2 in the order of seniority.

Logic for Solution: Here every person is to maximize his / her reward. Now let us see the reverse way. Let us name the persons in order of the seniority of their age as A, B, C, D and C. Now let us consider if in the process A, B and C are voted out and only D and E are left. Then whatever D distribute other than 0, 100 E will vote against as only E has the right of vote. Thus E will get all 100 and D would get nothing. Hence it is not in the interest of D to vote such that C is voted out when only three of them are remaining. Now let us consider what happens when only three persons C, D and E are remaining after A and B are voted out. Now C is the senior most and maximize his benefit. C will distribute the coins as 99, 1, 0. Now since 1 is better than nothing, D would vote in favour winning the decision by ensuring 50% votes. So C gets 99 coins D gets 1 coin and E gets nothing. Obviously E won't like this situation. Hence E will ensure that this situation won't arise. In other words E would not vote out B. Now go back to the situation when B was there. When B, C, D and E are there, B will distribute 97, 0, 2, 1. Now Dget 2 coins and E gets 1. Hence both D and E would vote in favour. This is better than the distribution of C in the next round if this distribution is voted out. With the vote of D and E in favour the distribution wins with votes more than 50% in favour of the the distribution. This is no good situation for C. So C won't like to reach this situation by voting out A. So C will ensure that A is not voted out. When all were in the game, A distributed as 97, 0, 1, 0, 2. This is a better situation for C and E than the next round. As we have seen that if A is eliminated, then in next round C gets nothing and E would get only one gold coin instead of two now. Hence C and E both will vote in favour. Thus the vote wins with 50% favourable votes. Hence the final distribution is 97, 0, 1, 0, 2 for A, B, C, D and E respectively.

133. Answer: m×n – 1 cuts.

Logic for Solution: Logic 1: First we need to take (m – 1) linear cuts to get m strips of n squares each. Now each of the m strips require (n − 1) linear cuts to get 1 × 1 squares out of all the strips. Number of these cuts is m×(n − 1). Thus the total number of linear cuts required is m×(n − 1) + (m − 1) = m×n − 1. Note that initially m was chosen arbitrarily. You can also start with n.

Logic 2: First linear cut splits the rectangle in two parts. Now any linear cut for any of the part splits that rectangle in two parts. In other words every line increases the number of rectangle by 1. Thus 1 cut makes the board in two parts, second cut makes the board in three parts and so on. Thus m×n − 1 linear cuts will split the board in m×n parts. Now we know that m×n size board has m×n number of 1 × 1 squares. Hence m×n − 1 linear cuts would cut the m×n board inpieces of 1 × 1 size.

134.   Answer: Probability is 2/3

Logic for Solution:

Logic 1: Since we got a Red ball in the first draw means the bag cannot be the one containing both White balls. So the possibility is it had both Red balls or one Red and one White balls. Now there are three balls in the possible two bags. Out of these two are Red. Hence possibility of the next ball to be Red is 2/3.

Logic 2: We use Baye's law of probability. The law states that,

$P(A\backslash B) = \frac{P(A \cap B)}{P(B)}$ It is read as Probability of event A when event B has taken place is equal to Probability of events A and B happening together divided by Probability of event B.

Thus, Probability of drawing second Red ball when first ball drawn from the same bag is Red is equal to Probability of drawing both Red balls from the same bag divided by Probability of drawing first ball as Red. Now let us find these probabilities.

Probability of drawing both Red balls from the same bag. Since out of three bags only one bag has both Red balls. Hence this probability is 1/3.

Probability of drawing first ball as Red. There are six balls and out of them three are Red. Hence this probability is 1/2. If anyone is too particular about probability theory we number the bags as 1, 2 and 3 with two White, one White and one Red, and Red balls. Then we can use addition and multiplication rule as,

Probability of drawing first ball as Red is equal to drawing first or second or third bag and then drawing the Red ball. For OR we use addition and for AND we use multiplication. Probability of drawing bag randomly is 1/3 for each bag and then probability of Red ball is 0, 1/2 and 1 respectively for the three bags. Hence the Probability of drawing first ball as Red is $\frac{1}{3} \times 0 + \frac{1}{3} \times \frac{1}{2} + \frac{1}{3} \times 1 = \frac{1}{2}$

Now, using Baye's rule, Probability of drawing second Red ball when first ball drawn from the same bag is Red = $\frac{1/3}{1/2} = \frac{2}{3}$

135. **Answer:** No one is closer as both are at the same place.

136. **Answer:** First take one linear cut passing through the center of the cake so that cake is cut in two equal parts. Then take another linear cut perpendicular to the first cut passing through the center of the cake. Now you have four pieces. Lastly take a horizontal linear cut such that the width (or height) of the cake is split in to two. Thus we will have eight pieces of cake, four at the bottom and four on the top. Well those who are weight conscious take bottom ones, you take top one with cream!

137. **Answer:** 2

Logic for Solution: Count shape of o in each number. That count is the answer.

To derive full benefit, do not refer to the answer unless you make enough efforts to solve the puzzle.

138. **Answer:** 0

Logic for Solution: Square of the first number minus square-root of the second number.

139. **Answer:** Y

Logic for Solution: Add the numbers and take last letter of the answer in word. For example first number 1+1+1+1 = 4 that is FOUR. So answer is R. Second sum of the numbers is EIGHT. So the answer is T. In this way 5+5+5+5 = 20 that is TWENTY. So the answer is Y.

140. **Answer:** 9919

Logic for Solution: First letter(s) indicates length of the word. Second letter(s) indicate number of month in calendar. Third letter(s) indicate alphabetic order count of the month. So September has 9 alphabets or its length is 9. It is 9th month of calendar. S counts 19th alphabet in the sequence of alphabets.

141. **Answer:** Playing chess.

Logic for Solution: As C was playing chess, there has to be other player with him.

142. **Answer:**

$28 = 1 + 9 + \sqrt{9} \times 6 = 1 + 9 + 3 \times 6 = 28$
$32 = -1 + \sqrt{9} \times 9 + 6 = -1 + 27 + 6 = 32$
$35 = -1 + (\sqrt{9} + \sqrt{9}) \times 6 = -1 + 6 \times 6 = 35$
$38 = 19 / (\sqrt{9} / 6) = 19 / (3 / 6) = 19 \times 2 = 38$
$72 = 1 \times (\sqrt{9} + 9) \times 6 = 12 \times 6 = 72$
$73 = 1 + (\sqrt{9} + 9) \times 6 = 1 + 12 \times 6 = 73$
$76 = 1 + (9 \times 9) - 6 = 1 + 81 - 6 = 76$
$77 = -19 + 96 = 77$
$100 = 1 + \sqrt{9} + 96 = 100$
$1000 = (1 + 9) \wedge (9 - 6) = 10 \wedge 3 = 1000$

143. **Answer:** 143547

Logic for Solution: first two numbers of the answer is the product of the first two terms of the question. Second two terms of the answer is the product of the first and the last term of the question. The last two terms of the answer is the sum of the first two terms and second two terms of the answer minus the middle term of the question.

Note: If a, b and c are the terms then it could be symbolically represented as,

$a + b + c = (a \times b)(a \times c)(a \times b + a \times c - b)$

144. **Answer:** Ages are Boy 7 year, Father 49 year and Grandfather 84 years

Logic for Solution: Let ages in years of the boy, father and grandfather be 'a', 'b' and 'c' respectively.

Now from the first statement we can wright the relationship as $12 \times a = c$

Also from the second statement we can wright the relationship as $7 \times a = b$

Also we know that $a + b + c = 140$

Substituting we get, the answer $a = 7$, $b = 49$, $c = 84$

145. **Answer:** 40 Cartons, This is more than 49% (almost 50%) of recycle saving to environment.

Logic for Solution: First the firm make 27 milk cartons by recycling 81 cartons. Then out of these 27 milk cartons firm makes 9 milk cartons by recycling. Then out of these 9 milk cartons firm makes 3 milk cartons by recycling. Then out of these 3 milk cartons firm makes 1 milk cartons by recycling. Thus total milk cartons produced by recycling from 81 used cartons is $27 + 9 + 3 + 1 = 40$

Percentage saving of environment is $(40/81) \times 100 = 49.3\%$

146. **Answer:** 15

Logic for Solution: let number of football players be 'n'. Let 'm_i' be the number of goals scored in world cup matches by the ith player. Number of goals they could have scored in world cup is 0, 1, 2, 3, ...etc. Now as per the condition c) $m_i <$ n for all i. Also by condition a $m_i \neq m_j$ for all i and j except i = j.

Hence only possible number of goals is 0, 1, 2, 3, ..., n which are 'n + 1' numbers for 'n' players. According to condition b) number of goals scored by any player cannot be 15. So the number of goals scored are 0, 1, 2, 3,........, 14, 16, ...n. Thus now there are 'n' numbers for 'n' players. But this is contradiction to the condition c). Thus with 14 players it is possible to have goals scored 0, 1, 2, 3, ...13 that satisfy all the conditions. Also with 15 players it is possible to have goals scored 0, 1, 2, 3, ...14 that satisfy all the conditions. However, with number of players 16 or more if the conditions a) and b) are satisfied, c) cannot be satisfied. Hence, maximum number of players is 15.

147. **Answer:** 15 + 9 + 6 or 13 + 11 + 6

Logic for Solution: All numbers are odd. Sum of three odd numbers is always odd. Hence we must have to use one even number. The only possible way is to use 6, which can be formed by rotating the given number 9. With using 6 we get multiple answers.

148. **Answer:** Reward was for saving his life. The sacking was for sleeping in the night shift when the watchman was supposed to be awake.

149. **Answer:** One of the doctor was woman, so they were three.

150. **Answer:** Coffin

151. **Answer:** There were only three persons. Man, his son and his grandson.

152. **Answer:** Bandu

Logic for Solution: Now by second statement Tina's husband is playing with Chandu's wife. This clearly indicates that Tina's husband cannot be Chandu or Candu's wife cannot be Tina. Further, if Tina's husband was Nandu, to satisfy both statements, there cannot be two pair with Nandu playing from both sides. Hence Tina must be Bandu's wife. Since Tina can play with Nandu both statements are satisfied.

153. **Answer:** 3 Hours

Logic for Solution: Since you as well as the bobber are floating in the river both are moving with the stream speed. So we ignore the speed of stream. Now the initial distance is 30 km between you and bobber. Your rowing speed is 10 km per hour. So you will take 3 hours to cover this distance.

www.ingramcontent.com/pod-product-compliance
Lightning Source LLC
Chambersburg PA
CBHW030938090426
42737CB00007B/469